Praise for

Through lyrical essays ̣ .. ..arp
and honest portrayal of what it means to navigate the strange corri-
dors of being diagnosed with chronic illnesses as a young woman, to
encounter the loss of a healthier self and some of the dreams that self
might have once had, to reconcile the values and mindsets of her
immigrant parents with the beliefs that are necessary to navigate life
in the United States, and to be proud in one's Afro-Latina identity
even if its location grounds it a geographic anomaly. Her stories are
at once gripping and achingly generous as she lays her life bare and
dissects what it means to be "Woman enough to wear the color of
blood and fire without fear and without trepidation."
— Elizabeth Acevedo, author of *The Poet X*

Jasminne Méndez's words are at once incandescent and scathing. Her
storytelling illumines the travails and the tenacity of a body bound
to—and unbound by—place, illness and history. Her language fills in
the synapses with the sweetness of mangoes, the soul of memory and
an unflinching eye for witness. Her pages elucidate American inter-
sectionality and bless all the overlooked songs.
— Barrie Jean Borich, author of *Apocalypse,*
Darling and *Body Geographic*

Growing up in Texas, the perspicacious child of Dominican immigrants,
Jasminne Méndez seems unstoppable, even when adulthood presents its
own set of challenges: a chronic illness, the anguish of pregnancy. The
bigger she dreams, the harder it becomes to love her body in this world.
But in her glorious book Méndez speaks her truth: an empowering journey of resilience, perseverance and the bittersweet wisdom that comes
from being the woman who has had to "learn to suck the nectar out of
sorrow."
— Rigoberto González, author of
What Drowns the Flowers in Your Mouth

Jasminne Méndez is a gift. End stop. In *Night Blooming Jasmin(n)e* you will find what no residency or workshop can teach: self-examination. Her writer's eye is unrelenting and compassionate. Where there are hereditary and genetic dispositions to blame, there are healings and epiphanies to celebrate. Using a fierce remedy of flash essays, personal narratives, poetry and musings, Méndez becomes our healer. Truly born of her blood, this debut is a beautiful achievement, a lasting testament to a spirit that emerged bruised, scarred but alive and ready to sing.

—Willie Perdomo, author of
The Essential Hits of Shorty Bon Bon

Jasminne Méndez's fearless debut, insists on two forms—straightforward, intimate first-person essays, interlaced with poems—as the modes necessary to write the rarity of her body urgently into existence: the Black Latinx body, the female body, the ill body, the infertile body. But also, beyond the fact of the body, the tender identities in-between: faithful daughter, brilliant student, brave patient, devoted wife, hopeful mother. These conversational, frank essays allow the reader into a life filled with love and family, but also incredible hardship, heartbreak and resilience. And the poems, woven wild as sprays of jasmine into the text, are, like the flower, sharp and flint-bright as stars, and vulnerable as its petals. Méndez is a bold, necessary voice from long-neglected intersections of experience. And, thank goodness, she has arrived.

—Vanessa Angélica Villarreal, author of *Beast Meridian*

NIGHT-BLOOMING JASMIN(N)E

PERSONAL ESSAYS AND POETRY

JASMINNE MÉNDEZ

Arte Público Press
Houston, Texas

Night-Blooming Jasmin(n)e is funded in part by grants from the City of Houston through the Houston Arts Alliance, the National Endowment for the Arts and the Texas Commission on the Arts. We are grateful for their support.

Recovering the past, creating the future

Arte Público Press
University of Houston
4902 Gulf Fwy, Bldg 19, Rm 100
Houston, Texas 77204-2004

Cover design by Mora Desıgn
Cover art by Esperanza Gama, "Mujer Fuego"
gamaesperanza@gmail.com

Names: Méndez, Jasminne, author.
Title: Night-blooming Jasmin(n)e : personal essays & poetry / by Jasminne Méndez.
Description: Houston, TX : Arte P?ublico Press, [2018]
Identifiers: LCCN 2017061347 (print) I LCCN 2018001715 (ebook) I
  ISBN 9781518504907 (epub) I ISBN 9781518504914 (kindle) I
  ISBN 9781518504921 (pdf) I ISBN 9781558858619 (alk. paper)
Subjects: LCSH: Scleroderma (Disease) I Scleroderma (Disease)—
  Anecdotes. I Pericardium—Diseases.
Classification: LCC RL451 (ebook) I LCC RL451 .M46 2018 (print) I
  DDC 616.5/44—dc23
LC record available at https://lccn.loc.gov/2017061347

18 19 20 21   5 4 3 2 1

For Lupe: my amo, my hands, my hero, my heart

TABLE OF CONTENTS

Night-Blooming Jasmin(n)e 1

PART I: SPANISH JASMIN(N)E

Loss 5
Independence 7
Exam Table 13
Diagnosis 14
Skin Score 39
Poet's Jasmin(n)e 54
Avalanche I 59
Hands Clean 60
When You Marry a Mexican American 62
Support Group 65

PART II: RED JASMIN(N)E

First Trimester 75
One in Four 76
Baby M 85
Not Yet 86
Insanity 88
What to Expect When You're Not Expecting ..89
Dar a Luz 90
How to Be Infertile 92
Open 98
Shades of Red 99
Waiting 104

PART III: SUMMER JASMIN(N)E

Gluttony: Undigested 109
Hunger 110
Interruptions 118
Lupus 121
ER Visits 122
"Sick" Humor 124
Young, Pretty & Able 132
Stroke 134
Mouth Sores 136
Mo(u)rning Medications 137
Detours 138
Inflammation 143
Heart 145

PART IV: WINTER JASMIN(N)E

Avalanche II 155
Hands: El Corte 156
Morir soñando 161
Hair 163
Massage Envy 167
Drop It 169
After the Avalanche 171

PART V: TRUE JASMIN(N)E

Hope 175
(W)Hole 185
Health 187
Home 198
Haima 203

Hostility 206
Heridas 211
Heroine 216

Acknowledgements 223
Gracias 225

NIGHT-BLOOMING JASMIN(N)E

This is the story   of Jasmin(n)e:
~~common~~ Jasmin(n)e   Spanish Jasmin(n)e
red Jasmin(n)e   ~~sweet~~ Jasmin(n)e
~~white~~ Jasmin(n)e   summer Jasmin(n)e
~~princess~~ Jasmin(n)e   true Jasmin(n)e
Jasmin(n)e tongue   Jasmin(n)e breath
Jasmin(n)e skin   Jasmin(n)e hair
Jasmin(n)e flowers   blooming inside
a Jasmin(n)e heart

PART I: SPANISH JASMIN(N)E

We were plucked
from our homes
& planted on foreign soil.
Wild—we grow
& flourish anywhere.

LOSS

I DON'T KNOW if I have the words I need to tell you everything I want to say. I don't know if I have enough creative impulses to get it all down on paper and truly convince you of my story. I don't really know where any of this is going. But I remember having dreams once. I remember believing in the impossible. I remember being someone else once. I don't know where she went. I think she died in the process. Between independence, diagnosis and disappointment, I've lost her somewhere. I tried to blame scleroderma. I tried to blame lupus. I tried to blame God. I tried to blame the world. But it's no one's fault. She couldn't take the pressure anymore. So she left.

The old me broke up with the new me and she left both of us broken-hearted. Imagine that, feeling the broken heart of two people at one time beating in your own chest. Grief becomes inevitable, depression a necessity.

I longed for the old me, like every lover does at the beginning of a separation. I went back to her time and time again. I begged for forgiveness. I promised to change. But nothing seemed to work. I spent hours and hours reliving her dreams, trying to believe in them again. But she and the dreams kept slipping away. I studied her face in old pictures and thought about how beautiful she was. I closed my eyes and remembered feeling safe and secure in her skin. I felt lost. I felt empty. I was afraid of being someone else. I had grown accustomed to her routine. She and I had wanted the same things before, had laughed at the same things before, believed in the same things

5

before. And yet, like every sad love affair that comes to an end, she left because what she needed and what I could give her no longer were the same, and the new me was left with the shattered pieces of a broken heart that didn't even exist.

INDEPENDENCE

I ASSERTED MY INDEPENDENCE from my strict and over protective father by refusing to graduate high school a year early, as he had wanted me to. Papi, my father, thought I wanted to stay in high school because of a boy. I actually wanted to stay in high school because attending college at sixteen seemed absurd. I just wasn't ready. I didn't want to grow up so fast. My whole life I was reaching milestones before everyone else. According to Mami, I potty-trained myself at age two by taking off my own diaper and running to the bathroom. At age four and a half, I threw a temper tantrum because I wanted to go to school but had to wait another year because I was born in November and no school would take me. In order to appease me, Papi, who worked at a hospital at the time, was able to somehow forge a birth certificate that said I was born in March rather than November. As a result, I started school early and was always younger than all of my peers. Throughout all my public school years, I was always seen as different because I was the black girl who spoke Spanish. Just this once, I didn't want to be different or exceptional, but Papi didn't understand that.

Papi believed that going to college early could secure my future. It meant having a "leg up" on everyone else, and Papi always said that because I was a woman of color, I would always have to try twice as hard to be considered half as good. But how could I worry about the future when I wasn't even able to create memories of my present? All I wanted were memories of going to prom, walking the stage in my cap and gown with my friends and attending a few more

7

football games and after-school drama practices. Memories that only
seemed to make sense to American high school kids, and that pover-
ty-stricken Dominican people like Mami and Papi didn't get the lux-
ury of having.

What I needed Papi to understand was that we didn't live in the
Dominican Republic anymore. I had grown up in America. We lived
in San Antonio, Texas. There was no place more American than
Texas, and I felt Papi needed to get with the program already. But
Papi's humble upbringing had made him practical. Papi knew that
memories didn't pay the bills or put food on the table. Papi wanted
me to have a financially secure future and stability; he made sure I
knew that a good education was the only way forward. I understood
that, but I decided that I could still have that AND a memorable senior year.

"Papi," I said as I found the courage to approach him one Saturday afternoon during the spring of my junior year of high school,
"Can I talk to you?" He had fallen asleep with the TV on. He opened
his eyes and sat up in the recliner when he heard my voice. Papi was
a large man. He was only about five and half feet tall when standing
at full attention, but his stern jaw, thick veiny hands and serious face
made him intimidating. As an Army sergeant, he always kept his hair
cut clean and was always in pretty good shape. Although he had pro-
cured a small beer belly in his older age, Papi was still strong as a
bear, not the kind of person one should bother while sleeping.

"¿Qué? What's the matter?" asked Papi sitting up startled.

"Can I talk to you?"

He sat up some more and wiped the crust from his eyes. "¿Qué
necesitas?"

"Nada. I just wanted to . . . " I hesitated. "I just wanted to tell
you that I've changed my mind about graduating early." I stared at a
stain in the rug and crossed my arms defensively.

"Why? We had a plan."

I could tell from his clenched jaw and stern cheeks that his blood
pressure was rising. My own body tensed up.

"I know, pero, I want to graduate with my friends. I don't want
to finish school so fast. I want to go to the prom."

The second the words left my mouth I knew he wouldn't understand. I knew he would think I was some lovesick teenager that had changed her mind because of a boy, even though I wasn't even allowed to date and had never brought a boy to the house.

The room went silent for a moment. Papi leaned back in his recliner and the leather creaked as it rubbed against his skin. "Fine. But don't expect me to help you with anything your senior year. I will sign whatever paperwork you need me to sign, but I'm not helping you get into or apply for college or scholarships. This is your decision, so you are responsible for it and you deal with the consequences."

"Okay," I sighed. "Fine. I understand. I'm sorry, Papi. I know you're disappointed, but this is what I want."

He reclined completely and closed his eyes.

I went outside and washed the car to try and atone for being such a disappointment. While scrubbing the windshield and hosing down the tires, I almost changed my mind. I almost ran back inside to say never mind, I'll do it if it'll make you happy. But then the thought of my own happiness stopped me. For once, I wanted to do what made me happy, even if it meant letting everyone else down. I continued scrubbing the car and my ego clean, knowing this small apologetic gesture would go unnoticed and unrewarded.

My father was a man of his word. All through my senior year, he barely said a word to me. He signed papers when I left them on the dining table and never asked me any questions or offered to help. And because mami stayed out of it. She refused to take sides, saying that it was between Papi and me. She wanted me to be happy, and deep down, I know she didn't want me going off to college so soon. And because Mami always tried to keep the peace in our house, she didn't ask me to reconsider, and she also didn't help me with any of my college or scholarship applications. Also her English was never that good, so she refused to sign anything if she didn't know what it was for.

That next year, I spent hours each month filling out applications, stuffing envelopes with transcripts, resumés and essays. I even created a color-coded file folder of all the schools and scholarships I applied to. I knew someone would give me money and I would be going to college. I was a smart student with good grades. I took several advanced placement classes, participated in drama, band and speech, and I had glowing recommendation letters from all of my teachers. Deep inside I knew staying for my senior was the best decision I had made. I just needed one acceptance letter and a great scholarship to prove it to Papi.

By early spring of my senior year, I had applied to five state schools and over thirty scholarships. When Papi saw all the work I was putting into my college application process, and he realized that I wasn't a boy-crazy, lost cause, he started talking to me again and taking an interest in what I was doing.

"¿Cómo te va?" he asked one Sunday afternoon as I sat in the middle of my room surrounded by pink, yellow and blue file folders.

"Bien. I think." I was working on a few more scholarship applications because I had only received a $1000 scholarship, which I knew would barely pay for books at San Antonio College.

"Me alegro que lo estés tomando en serio. If you want, we can visit some of the schools you got accepted to. So you can see them and decide where you want to go."

I knew he was throwing me a bone, and I really did want to go visit the schools that had accepted me. But I was my father's daughter, and I was just as stubborn as he was.

"Maybe. Yeah, we can talk about it, but I'm just really busy with all this paperwork and school. I'll let you know."

"Okay. It would be a good idea for you to see where you're going before you go," he insisted.

"Yeah. I know, Papi. Gracias."

I looked back down at my file folders, and he left the room head down, hands in his pockets, rejected.

By the time graduation rolled around, so had Papi and I. Even though I still had no clue how I was going to pay for college because, while my friends received full and partial scholarships to the universities of their choice, I had yet to receive anything more than $1000. Mami, Papi and I had visited several colleges, and I had fallen in love with the University of Houston. It was far enough from my parents, but close enough for them to come visit whenever they wanted. It wasn't an expensive school, but it was more than we could afford. Papi had decided that I could spend the first two years of college at home with them, save money and then transfer to UH for the last two years. Logistically and financially, I knew that was my best option, but emotionally I didn't want to stay in San Antonio a minute longer. I had to get out of that town. I had to get out of my parent's house. I needed my freedom, and I wanted to have the real college experience I was promised by my American teachers in my American high school.

It was almost July when I began to lose hope of ever leaving home for college. I either hadn't heard from or had been rejected by the scholarship organizations I applied to. My future seemed bleak, and I began to wonder if staying for senior year to create memories with friends I would probably never see again was worth it.

At the end of July, I finally saw a light at the end of the tunnel. Since January of that year, I had checked the mailbox every day in the hopes that I would find an acceptance letter or a scholarship offer. In June, I had received noticed from the Bill Gates Millenium Fund that I was a semi-finalist for their scholarship award, but I hadn't understood what that meant because the application never indicated how much the scholarship was for. I was excited and I told Papi, but since being a semi-finalist wasn't a sure thing, I didn't let myself get excited about it. Then in late July, when I checked the mail and saw that it was from the Gates Foundation, I ripped the envelope open, read the first few lines and screeched. I ran back to the house, slid into to the kitchen and showed Papi that I was a finalist for the Bill Gates Millennium Scholarship Award.

"¡Papi! ¡Mira! Look, I'm a finalist. They say they will pay for EVERYTHING, for all four years!"

"¿Qué? ¿De verdad?" His face beamed. His jaw stood agape and his cheeks swelled with pride.

"Sí. Yes. I just have to keep 'good academic standing.'"

"Qué bueno. Qué bueno," he repeated over and over and patted me on the back.

I wrapped my arms around him, and we would've cried if Papi had been a man for tears. But his acceptance and pride in me were more than enough. I knew he wouldn't have to worry about me, after all. I knew I was going to be all right. I knew he believed in me again, and I did too.

EXAM TABLE

pink paper patient
lie back and get comfortable
fade into the "thank you"
and the "how are you feeling"
and the "does that hurt" dandelion
dissonance that flurries over
your sunflower breasts and
wooden windchime legs
slip the wheek of a guinea pig
between your tongue and teeth
hide it with a hand or a hiccup
remind yourself you are human
even if this won't change
the weather or the results
the diagnosis or the disease
that winters your summer skin

DIAGNOSIS

SCLERODERMA isn't something you prevent; it's something that happens. Scleroderma has no known specific cause, origin or cure. Scleroderma means survival, which does not always equate to living.

Scleroderma is:
   heavy joints on a rainy day that keep you from washing your hair or brushing your teeth or opening a jar.
Scleroderma is:
   diarrhea in the middle of the night that rips your insides and won't stop leaking out of you until your whole world spins.
Scleroderma is:
   cold fingers on a lukewarm day that keep you from signing a check or driving in to work on time.
Scleroderma is:
   thick skin stretched so taut you become a wax museum replica of who you used to be.
Scleroderma is:
   a nine-hour nap in the middle of the day because your body weighs more than your desire to be productive.
Scleroderma is:
   a tender touch from your lover that feels like a thousand needles on your skin.
Scleroderma is:
   heartburn at 2 pm that lasts until 9 am the next morning.
Scleroderma is:
   excess collagen coating your arms, shins, chest, neck and face.

Scleroderma is:
fibrosis in the lungs and labored breathing.
Scleroderma is:
anxiety.
Scleroderma is:
depression.
Scleroderma is:
fatigue.
Scleroderma is:
chronic.

I

It was November of 2006. I was on the phone with my boyfriend, Lupe, bringing in a bag of groceries. I was complaining about grad school again, and he was patient and attentive like a priest during confession. I dropped my purse on the couch as I entered my one-bedroom apartment and headed to the kitchen with my bag of poultry and vegetables. As I laid the bag on the counter, my fingers emerged from the plastic, and what I saw confused me.

"What the hell?" I stopped and turned my left hand back and forth.

"What? What happened? Are you okay?" Lupe asked.

"Um, I'm not sure. I just set down this bag of groceries and now my hands are all white."

"What do you mean?"

"I mean they're white. Like pale, stone-cold white. And they're kinda numb."

"Do they hurt?"

"No. But, hey, let me let you go. I gotta do something about this. And I gotta put these groceries away."

"Okay, love you. Call me when you're done."

"Yeah, love you too."

I hung up the phone and stared at both my hands, perplexed. They felt cold, so I ran them under hot water. In a few minutes the numbness faded and they had returned to a bright red color. I didn't give it a second thought.

What I had experienced then and would continue to do so for the next few months before going to the doctor was Raynaud's phenomenon. It was the first noticeable symptom I remember. Raynaud's is characterized by a feeling of numbness in the extremities, hands and feet. It is usually caused by cold temperatures or stress. The fingers and toes turn white and often ache and tingle until they are warmed up. As the digits regain feeling, they turn blueish purple and then finally red. Severe Raynaud's can lead to ulcers, which, if left untreated, can lead to gangrene and eventually the removal of the digit.

Although I did not worry much about that episode, I continued to have them throughout that winter. So, in January of 2007, I decided to visit my doctor and find out why I had bad circulation, which was what both my family and I assumed it was.

I didn't have my own doctor at the time because I was the kind of person who never got sick, not even a cold or flu. I was always strong and healthy. The last time I had seen a doctor was for a sprained ankle back when I was in high school and still lived at home with my parents. I asked Lupe for the name of his doctor and scheduled an appointment.

"So what's going on?" asked Dr. Rogers, a middle-aged black woman with ruby red lips, big hair and wide hips.

"Well, every time I'm cold, my fingers turn white. And they hurt and tingle until the blood comes back. It's something to do with bad circulation, right?"

"Hmm. Lay back."

She began the routine examination that I would eventually be able to predict like a sitcom rerun. First she checked the sound of my lungs, then the beating of my heart. She placed her fingers on my throat, then looked into my eyes, ears, nose and mouth. She pinched my fingers and toes and massaged the back of my neck.

"Can you make it happen?"

"What do you mean?"

"Can you make your hands turn white?" She shrugged as if what she had said should make perfect sense to me.

"Um, no, I don't think so. It's just when I'm cold."

I was confused as to why she would assume that I could force my fingers into numbness and discoloration, and/or why I would even want to if I could. As if what was happening to me were some kind of magic trick.

"Hmm. Okay, well, we'll run some bloodwork and see what happens. Is there anything else?" She flipped through her chart and walked towards the door.

I fiddled with my jeans. "No. I don't think so."

At that point I didn't know that it was important to tell her that I could take a five-hour nap and still feel tired or that my body always felt like it had just finished training for the Olympics. I was a full-time grad student, a full-time volunteer coordinator with the department of education and I was always auditioning for and rehearsing for local community theatres. I figured it was natural that I would feel tired all the time. So I didn't say anything else, and she left the room and told me to meet the nurse outside.

The nurse, a kind, overweight red-faced, Latina guided me to the blood draw station and told me to sit down, roll up my sleeve and open and close my fist. I complied. I was never really afraid of needles, so the actual blood draw didn't bother me at first. But I began to get really concerned as the blood kept flowing and the jolly nurse kept filling up vile after vile with my blood.

"Wow," I said, "that's a lot of blood." I was beginning to get faint, but only because the sight of that much blood coming out of me seemed unreal.

"Oh, m'ija, it's really not that bad." She smiled big, her full pink lips stretching across her face, revealing lipstick on her teeth and making her nose hairs emerge slightly. Her gleeful appearance made me chuckle nervously.

"If you say so."

"Just relax. We're almost done."

Eight large and three small vials later, she handed me a cup and told me to go to the bathroom. "Just close the lid tightly and leave it on the counter by the sink when you're finished. Come to the front desk when you're all done, and the receptionist will check you out."

"Thanks."

I took the cup, went to the bathroom and handled my business. It wasn't the first time I'd had to pee in a cup for a doctor, but I was really curious as to just how much of my bodily fluids this doctor needed from me simply because of cold hands.

"All done?" asked the grey-haired African American receptionist at the counter.

"I guess so."

"All right, hun, you're all set then. You paid your co-pay when you came in, right?"

"Um, yeah. The twenty-five dollars?" I hesitated because the language of insurance companies, with words like "co-pay," "deductible" and "premiums," were still foreign to me. I had a hard time differentiating what I had to pay, when and to whom.

She smiled as if she could see the angst in my face, patted my hand like Mami did when she was trying to reassure me and said, "Yep."

I sighed and smiled back. "Okay, then yeah, I did."

"Then you're all set." She handed me the paperwork that would only be the beginning to the tall stack of papers I would eventually collect and file away for future reference. "The doctor will call you if she needs to see you again. Otherwise, you'll get the results in the mail in five to ten business days."

"Okay. Thank you." I walked out of the anti-bacterial, germ-free office ready for a nap.

"How'd it go?" asked Lupe when I called him from the car.

"Eh. They took a lot of blood, I peed in a cup and they said they would call me if it was anything to worry about."

"How do you feel?"

"Tired."

I went home and fell asleep.

A week later I returned to Dr. Rogers' office because the nurse had called and told me to come in. The doctor needed to review the results of my bloodwork. I was anxious when I arrived at the clinic and I couldn't stop fidgeting with my clothes while I waited in the exam room. When Dr. Rogers entered the room, she didn't waste time with formalities. She got straight to the point.

"You have lupus," said Dr. Rogers. She shook her head disapprovingly. "How old are you?"

"Twenty-two," I replied as the implications of what she had just said bounced around in my skull and made my head spin.

"Hmm. So young."

My feet dangled back and forth off the exam table. I rubbed my legs and exhaled.

"So, what do I do now? I mean, what does that mean?"

"Well, I'm going to refer you to a specialist. A good friend of mine. He's a rheumatologist; he can help you manage this disease. Lupus is a chronic autoimmune disease that usually affects women. Now, this illness can take on many different forms and may even affect your internal organs, but that's not something you should worry about just yet. Although there is no known cause or cure, there are many treatments available. If you take care of yourself properly, you can expect to live a relatively normal life. Do you have any questions?"

I sat there and stared at her, still trying to process all of the complicated words that shot out from her mouth like bees stinging me with every syllable. I didn't want to cry, yet. I didn't feel angry, yet. I didn't even feel confused. My brain and my heart, at the moment, like my hands a few months before, began to feel numb.

"You'll want to stay away from sugar, fatty foods, excessive sodium and carbohydrates. Certain foods can aggravate the condition. You'll also want to rest frequently and take a daily vitamin until you can get the medication you need from the rheumatologist."

"Okay," was all I could mutter. It was all I felt.

She patted me on the shoulder, smiled in a bedside manner kind of way and walked out of the room. The pink-lipped nurse came to the room, guided me to a small office and handed my file to a clerk.

"She's going to set up the appointment with the specialist for you, m'ija. Just have a seat." She patted me on the shoulder and left the room.

"How are you today?" asked the twenty-something handsome clerk in bright blue scrubs with bright blue eyes and dark hair.

"I'm fine, thanks," I said, clutching my purse and looking every-where else but at him. Making eye contact with anyone at that point seemed deceptive.

"So, what day works for you?"

"Um, I don't know. When can he see me?"

"Well, he has Monday the first at 9 am or Wednesday the third at two."

I searched the calendar in my head. I decided 9 am would be best so that I wouldn't have to mull it over all day and I told him to pencil me in.

"Okay, sounds great then, Ms. Rosario. 9 am on Monday it is."

"Thank you."

I walked out of the office and into the parking garage. I sat in my car, adjusted the rearview mirror, saw my blank reflection in the windshield and began to cry. The next day, Saturday morning, I put on my cap and gown, walked the stage and received my Masters degree in education. What was supposed to have been the beginning of my adult life in the real world felt more like the end.

II
"Disappointment"

After the initial misdiagnoses of lupus, which was quickly re-diagnosed as scleroderma, I decided to quit my full-time job with benefits and pursue my real dreams. The two degrees I had earned over the last five years on my full scholarship were for my father. I was still trying to prove to him that I would be okay on my own. I knew my education was "algo que nadie te puede quitar," something I would have "para siempre." And since I had achieved Papi's goals of earning both an undergraduate and a graduate degree, it was now time for me to achieve my own goals.

I decided that I was going to make a living off my art. I was going to do this by teaching part-time, working as a writer and working on paid acting gigs wherever I could. At twenty-two, I had no real plan as to how I was going to pay my bills, get health insurance and the medication I didn't realize I would need every month. I had saved enough money from my full-time job to live carefree for at least three months while I tried to figure things out. What I needed most right then was time to rest. I needed time to think and be with myself. I couldn't do that with the full-time job I loathed, so I quit. The non-profit salaried job with benefits had kept me confined to a dreary cubicle five days a week. It was, I believed, the reason for my current health crisis. My body was ailing because my spirit was broken by the soulless mundane work I did every day. As I look back on it now, quitting my job was just the first step towards quitting my whole life.

During my time of "self-discovery," I gained twenty pounds, lost contact with all of my close friends and sent Mami and Papi into a mad frenzy of denial, anger, confusion and sadness. At the time, I assumed their grief was my fault, since I was the one who was sick. But I know now that, just as I had to come to terms with my illness, those I loved had to trudge the murky waters of grief for themselves too.

I tried several physical and emotional remedies. I self-medicated hoping to heal my fractured self. I tried to write, but everything sounded like a cheap self-help novel of navel-gazing antidotes and dismissive platitudes. I tried acupuncture for insomnia, fatigue, heartburn and pain but realized quickly that I couldn't afford the weekly treatments. I tried to self-medicate with alcohol, but it only made my joints swell and my muscles ache even worse. I tried to tap into higher realms of consciousness and being with marijuana, but it only made me sleepy, and when I slept, I dreamed of running and swimming and dancing, activities I could no longer do without feeling pain and fatigue. My dreams bullied me and left me feeling bruised and beaten. I tried to seek actual medical help from a doctor, but she wanted to medicate my depression with Prozac and Xanax. She said the pills would make it better. But I knew she was talking about the fog and apathy and not the actual physical pain that stretched across every cell of my body. I threw the prescriptions out, deciding that the fog would lift when the physical pain lessened. I still believed that this was just a phase, and I would get better soon.

Despite my best efforts, my depression intensified. I lived in a gray haze of over-eating and restless fatigue. I would scream when I couldn't lift my arms to put my hair up in a ponytail. I crumbled to the tiled floor in the bathroom and cried when day after day I couldn't make it out of the shower without stopping to catch my breath. I canceled plans with friends, hoping the fatigue would lessen. I sobbed like a busted fire hydrant as I got up every morning and the illness was still just as suffocating and debilitating as the morning before. Almost no one knew the extent of what I was really going through, and every day the unbearable fatigue that accompanied the illness grew worse because the immuno-suppresant drugs I was on didn't actually seem to suppress anything. I was only working part-time, as I had planned, but I had three odd jobs in different non-profits. The only steady income I had was working as an adjunct faculty member at the local community college. After paying my bills, I survived on three hundred dollars every two weeks. But somewhere, deep inside me, the old me, the pre-scleroderma me, believed that life as a starving artist was okay because I was living the dream, and I still held the belief that anything was possible.

Mami and Papi didn't know that I had quit my full-time-with-benefits dream job. I was too afraid to tell them. I didn't want them to think I was a failure. I didn't want them to worry about me not having health insurance. I didn't want to disappoint them because I knew they wouldn't understand my desire to achieve a dream that had no "real" future, just like Papi hadn't understood my American high school dream of going to the prom and graduating with my friends. So, from June to November of 2007, I avoided the conversation of my job. When my savings ran out, my electricity got cut off and my stomach growled, I let my pride keep me company.

I refused to ask Mami and Papi for a dime. I didn't need them to feel like their efforts to help me achieve a better life than the one they had were all for naught. I was supposed to be the responsible child. The one who could take care of them in their old age. We all understood this; it was an unspoken truth for my two siblings and me. Of the three of us, I was the most practical and resourceful. I hadn't depended on Mami and Papi in years and I wasn't about to start then. After I graduated high school and went to college with a full scholarship, I didn't need to depend on them anymore. I set my own rules and didn't ask for money or advice. When in crisis, everyone called *me* for advice and/or money. I was the one who was supposed to have it "all together."

I couldn't let them know that I wanted and needed to be selfish in order to pursue pipe dreams with no guaranteed financial gain. I couldn't reveal that I was squandering away my degrees on art and on what Papi had always referred to as "tu hobby." So I kept my silence and lied by omission. This was difficult because Mami called me every day just to "saber como seguía." It was a nice gesture and I knew she meant well, but she always asked about work and I always had to lie. Our conversations became tiresome and draining. I was not sure how much longer I could keep them from the truth.

One afternoon while suffering from another bout of heartburn and indigestion, I received a call from Mami that turned into an attempt to assert her authority over my life and make demands.

"Vamos contigo a tu próxima visita con el doctor," Mami said with the same tone she used to take when ordering me to clean my room.

"But why? I don't need you to come with me. I'll be fine." I whined like a spoiled child with better things to do.

I knew this whining wouldn't stop them from coming, but I didn't want them driving the three and half hours from San Antonio to Houston just to ask more questions and find out what I had been hiding for almost six months.

"No debes de ir al doctor sola. Y además, tu papá sabe qué preguntarle al doctor."

I could hear pots and pans banging in the background. I knew she was making dinner for Papi. It was almost six and Papi would be home from work soon, demanding la bandera: arroz, habichuelas y carne. Suddenly, I was hungry. Although I didn't want her, and especially not Papi in my business, asking the doctor unnecessary and embarrassing questions, I yearned for a good home-cooked meal. I began to imagine a plate full of Mami's warm rice and beans drizzled with salsita from the pollo guisado or marinated beef tips. I wanted her to know how much I missed her cooking and the smells of Pine-Sol and garlic in the kitchen. I knew how happy it would make her to hear me say "extraño tu comida." But I kept this to myself because it would break her heart to know I needed her and she was so far away, and because she had raised me to be strong and independent and "fine." And right then, I needed both of us to be fine.

"Mami, I don't want Papi here making assumptions and questioning the doctor. Papi thinks he knows everything but he doesn't." I sighed into the phone and opened and closed my own kitchen cabinets searching for food that wouldn't make my indigestion or heartburn worse.

"Vamos a ir." She insisted they'd come. "¿Okay? Además, yo no quiero que andes manejando sola en la calle."

I heard oil sizzling in the background and my stomach grumbled.

"Mami, what do you mean you don't want me driving by myself? Why? I drive to work every day just fine."

I was genuinely confused by her desire to drive me to my doctor's appointment since I had not given her any indication that I was disabled or handicapped in any way. My hands and feet still worked, and I drove myself every day. Her over-protectiveness was exhausting, and I wanted to get off the phone so I could find something to eat and lie down.

"Tú te cansas fácil. No discutas conmigo." That was an order: don't argue!

I heard sizzling again in a pan on the other end. I imagined plantains or onions and garlic sautéing for the *sofrito*. I could almost smell Mami's cooking. My stomach groaned again and I wanted her in my kitchen cooking and feeding me towards better health. I decided then that I wanted a plate of Mami's food more than I cared about my own personal space and independence, so I acquiesced to her demands.

"Fine, Mom, you and Papi can come. But I have things to do, so you can't stay all weekend. The appointment is at 11 am on Friday."

"Cuídate. Bendición. Te quiero mucho."

"Love you too, Mom," I said and realized that we'd only begun to say these words of love and kindness post my diagnosis. It was as if we were both afraid I was dying and we had to make up for lost time.

I hung up the phone and was suddenly filled with panic. The appointment had been scheduled months ago, when I still had health insurance and a steady paycheck. My mind flooded with questions that tightened my chest. How the hell was I going to pay for this visit without insurance? How the hell was I going to pay for any new medications the doctor would inevitably prescribe? How on God's green earth was I going to continue lying to my parents about it all? Mami and Papi deserved the truth, but I was too weak and too scared and too tired to give it to them. I called Lupe in an attempt to find comfort.

"What should I do?" I asked him after I told him that Mami insisted they come with me to the next appointment.

"You should have told them months ago, like I said in the first place," he said matter-of-factly.

"Yeah, well I didn't. So now what?"

"Tell them on Friday when they get here before the appointment."

"Ugh, no I can't do that. Then they'll want to pay for everything."

"And what's so bad about that?"

"I can't depend on them. Then they'll think they can control me and that I'm a disappointment. They'll think they have to mantenerme like they do my brother and sister. I can't do that to myself or to them."

"Amor, just tell them already. It'll be fine. They're you're parents and they'll love you no matter what."

"You're no help. You don't know my dad. He's gonna throw a fit and tell me I have two degrees and that I should use them. That I'm wasting my talent and that I didn't think things through. You don't get it. Anyway, I gotta go. I need to find something to eat. I love you."

I hung up the phone, out of breath, my heart trying to pound its way out of my chest, more fatigued than before. I gave up on food and cooking, left the pots out, empty like my stomach, and decided to take a nap instead. Hoping that when I awoke, the answer to what I should do when my parents arrived would be clear.

≥ ≥ ≥

"How was the drive?" I asked Papi when they got out of the car and came towards me ready to hug, grateful that I didn't look as bad as they had expected. That morning, I was able to put my hair up in a ponytail—a dramatic feat only I had celebrated with glee—and I was wearing jeans and a blouse Mami had given me for my birthday, simply so she wouldn't think I hated it or had given it away. I hugged Papi, and he grabbed my arms to look for scars and thickening skin.

"Hola, Yamina," he said as he squeezed my forearms, sore and itchy from the excess collagen coating my skin like a thin, melted layer of candle wax that would eventually stiffen and lead to limited mobility.

"How are you?" he asked, peering above his gold-rimmed glasses, trying to find more signs of illness in my face, neck and chest.

"I'm okay," I replied, pulling away and feeling violated by this sudden invasion.

He pinched my face and squeezed my shoulders. This sent a shooting pain down my arms. I was extra sensitive; pain would pulse through every joint and hair follicle on my body, even without being touched, so his attempt at tenderness was met with a strong aversion rather than love. I flinched and backed away from him.

"Dad, stop. I'm fine. It's just like it was before."

I kept backing away as my body throbbed at the shoulders. I massaged my arms and shoulders to release his invasive, piercing touch from my skin.

"But how are you feeling?" he persisted, walking towards me. "Does it feel like it's getting any better? Are you taking your medicine every day?" He began waving his hands wildly in the air, trying to make sense of what the doctors didn't even fully understand.

I dismissed him. "Yes, yes, yes. Can we go inside now?"

I turned around and, as we walked into the building, I hugged Mami. She smiled apologetically for Papi's behavior, but also for me and my condition and the fact that for the first time in my life, she felt helpless.

"Te quedó bien la blusa," she said, looking at the blouse and pulling me in close with her soft hand.

I nestled my head in the crook of her neck and shoulder. Mami was about half a foot smaller than me, so I had to bend down and lean in close. Her dark-brown, shoulder-length hair tickled my cheek. She smelled of her Paris perfume. It was light like fresh tulips and a hint of honey. I was warmed by her embrace, and Papi's cold hands suddenly became a distant memory. I always yearned for this kind of affection and love from Mami, but her opinions and criticisms of my life had always kept me at a distance. I never felt like I could do enough or be enough for her. It always seemed like she wanted me to be more Dominican, more domestic, more like her and less like me. But lately, since my diagnosis, every time she saw me, she was kind and gentle, warm and motherly.

We walked into the clinic, which was painted in a dated jade color. A beige carpet covered every inch of the floor, floral plastic armchairs lined the walls and mahogany brown side tables filled the corners. The waiting room was crowded with patients older than even Mami and Papi. I shouldn't be here, I thought. I was too young to be this sick. I was too young to feel this tired. I believed I didn't have enough age in my bones for them to feel this heavy. The other patients stared at me as my parents sat down and I walked up to the counter, willing my hips and legs to move normally so as not to reveal how much pain I was in and make Mami worry. I was also taking my time because I knew I didn't have insurance anymore and was dreading the out-of-pocket self-pay expenses. My heart was ready to run out of my chest, my fingers twitched and my mouth was dry. I tried to smile as I approached the check-in desk.

"Hello, good morning," I muttered.

"Good morning, hun. Who are you here to see today?" asked the stout but friendly Latina receptionist with large hoop earrings and blue contacts.

"Dr. Malloy." I averted her eyes for fear she'd be able to tell I was uninsured.

"Okay, hun, sign in and let me see your ID and insurance card." Her smile lit up the room for a moment as she extended her freshly manicured hand.

I fumbled through my purse, opened my wallet and, with trembling fingers, handed her the insurance card from my previous job. I wanted to vomit. The smell of rubbing alcohol and bleach from the clinic made my head spin. I knew what I was doing was wrong. I knew I no longer had coverage, but I couldn't risk my parents finding out and causing a scene. The receptionist with the big hair and plastic nails took my card, looked at the papers in my file and handed it back to me.

"Any changes to your information? Name, address, telephone number, insurance?" Her eyebrows furrowed and she cocked her head to the side, her large earrings resting on her shoulders catching the light. I blinked hard.

"No," I lied, avoiding her eyes again and pretending to look for something in my purse.

"Okay, hun. You're all set then. The nurse will call you in a few."

"Thank you." I walked back to where Mami and Papi sat, still rummaging through my purse as if looking for redemption at the bottom.

"¿Todo bien?" Mami asked, looking up from a *Diabetes Today* magazine.

"Yeah, everything's fine," I replied, sounding chipper and hopeful.

As soon as I sat down, the receptionist called my name. "Ms. Jasminne."

I froze. I clutched my purse in fear. I assumed the worst. She must have looked up my insurance. She must have realized I was no longer covered. I panicked, realizing that I was probably going to go to jail for insurance fraud. I couldn't move. Mami looked up at me and then at the receptionist. I tried to swallow the guilt, but it got stuck in my throat.

"Ms. Jasminne?" she said again, looking around at everyone in the waiting room.

Papi stood up this time and began to walk toward the counter. I came back to life and edged past him, reaching the counter just seconds before he did. I motioned for him to sit down and mouthed, "Está bien, siéntate" before he could ask any questions.

"Um, yes, that's me. What is it?" I twisted the handle of my purse, writhing it in my hands, my breath becoming shorter and my jaw clenching. I felt someone following me. When I turned around, Papi was standing behind me.

"Papi, have a seat, I can handle this."

He stood firm as if he didn't understand my orders.

I turned back to the receptionist.

"Ma'am, we just need your $35 specialist co-pay, that's all." She smiled. I breathed hard and tried to smile back.

"Oh, okay. Papi, please go sit down."

I shooed him away, and he left reluctantly, putting his hands in his pockets and shaking his head like a lonely kid at recess. I handed the woman my debit card and prayed while the machine dialed numbers and made noises, that the card would be accepted because I was not even sure I had $35 to my name. The receipt printed, my shoulders relaxed, I signed the receipt and sat back down.

"¿Como está el trabajo?" Mami asked while licking her fingers and flipping through a magazine she could barely read because it was in English. She didn't think her question was out of the ordinary and it was her way of initiating conversation, since we were all trying to hide the fact that we were afraid of what the doctor might tell us this time.

I wanted to keep this conversation short and simple because I didn't want to have to lie more than what I needed to. I replied succinctly: "It's fine."

She didn't look up from her pretend reading and continued her line of questioning. She asked if they let me take the whole day off or if I had to go in after my appointment. I remained silent for too long, so she looked up from the magazine and stared at me. I stared at an artificial plant across the room that somehow looked wilted and sad.

"¿Yamina?" She placed her vanilla-smelling hand on my shoulder.

I turned to look at her, and the guilt swelled up inside me. I almost began to cry. I swallowed hard and held my breath.

"I have the whole day off." I said and shrugged her hand off of me so I could feel less remorse.

I started cleaning out my purse. "Wow, look at all this. I need to clean this thing out more often," I said, trying to change the subject. I pulled out old receipts, sticky coins, candy wrappers and a few bobby pins. I was trying desperately to distract us both from the inevitable disaster this uneasy conversation was going to lead us to.

"Dámelos." Mami took the bobby pins out of my hand and pulled her short black hair out of her face. "¿Ves?" she asked, smiling to show off her new do.

The conversation about my current employment status had been successfully delayed for now, and I was able to breathe a little easier.

About a half hour later, a short but very buff and handsome male nurse emerged from an inconspicuous door in the front of the room. He held a brown clipboard in his right hand and a bright-orange pen in his left. He called my name. I got up, determined to make this visit as quick and painless as possible. As I approached him, I noticed that his orange scrubs were too small for his muscular frame. They hugged his biceps and pulled tight around his pecks. I could see his nipples hardened by the cold AC air blasting in the waiting room. My nerves relaxed, and I brightened as soon as he smiled at me, his olive skin and defined cheekbones too GQ for such a thankless job like nursing at a rheumatologist's office. I walked up to the door and imagined him posing shirtless on the cover of a magazine. Mami and Papi trailed behind me like a pair of stray cats. I felt their presence warming the back of my neck.

"Are these your parents?"

"Yes," I replied embarrassed that, as a grown woman, I needed my parents to come with me to the doctor. But I knew that if I asked them to stay in the waiting room, they would feel hurt. After all, they didn't drive three and half hours to wait outside. My guilt won, and I asked the nurse if they could come in with me.

"Of course. Right this way."

The four of us walked into another room that was even colder and emptier than the first. The nurse took my temperature, pulse and blood pressure. All was normal. He told me to stand on the scale, at which point my pleasant disposition vanished. I ask him not to say the number out loud. This made us both laugh, and I felt at ease again. He told us to have a seat and that the doctor would be in shortly. Papi thanked him as he left. My anxiety began to bubble up again. I fidgeted with my purse.

As we waited, time seemed to be taking two steps forward and one step back. Mami flipped through a magazine, and Papi paced the tiny exam room. There were two arm chairs, one medical table with the typical white scratchy paper sheet draped over it to keep everything sanitary, a stainless steel sink and a gray countertop covered with glass bottles of cotton balls, popsicle sticks (tongue depressors) and Q-tips. Three people in this room made it feel crowded, and Papi's pacing two steps forward and three steps back made it feel like the walls were closing in on me.

"What is taking them so long?" Papi asked, as usual unable to wait for anything.

He stepped outside the room, looked around and asked, "Hey, what's going on? It's been over an hour. Did they forget about us?"

The nurse mumbled something about a busy day and to be patient, but my father was not satisfied with the response. Mami had resorted to picking at and chewing on her hair, a nervous habit she'd perfected over the years when faced with stressful situations.

"Papi, calm down. They'll be here soon," I said, trying to calm my own nerves.

The waiting made my legs shake and my back ache from sitting in the cold, hard plastic chair. I stood up and told Papi to sit for a while, and he actually complied. Then *I* started pacing. Another 30 minutes passed. I had read and reread every skeleton and "this is how your nerve system works" poster in the room over a dozen times. I was tired of waiting. I was nervous. I was annoyed.

"Ms. Rosario . . . " The doorknob finally turned and a Louis Armstrong look-alike walked through the door, saying my name as he reviewed my chart and faked a smile. Tired, he said, "Sorry for the wait, we're swamped."

He looked like a gentle old man. Average height, a trimmed cut with edges so clean I could tell he was a barber shop regular. He had a wide nose and a soft wrinkled face with a round mustache. His shirt was well-pressed, and he wore a tie underneath his white lab coat. He was the type of black man that I believed, like Papi, played dominoes with his friends on the weekend. He probably hosted a crawfish boil on his patio every year, and had grandchildren and a wife with a quaint house in one of the older suburbs. I imagined he could even pass for one of my grandfathers were it not for his thick southern drawl.

I deduced that he was the kind of doctor that didn't earn as much as he could because he'd chosen to open his private practice in the predominantly black side of town, where most of his patients were either on Medicaid/Medicare or uninsured like me. He apologized again for the delay as he took my hand and reintroduced himself as Dr. Malloy.

"Nice to see you," I said and shook his hand.

"And you're her parents, I assume." He turned to look at Mami and Papi, who were also smiling.

"Yes," said Papi, and he and Mami shook the doctor's hand.

"I'm Doctor Malloy, nice to meet you both. Now, let's see, last time you were here we diagnosed you with scleroderma. And we prescribed Naproxen for the pain and Protonix for the heartburn. How's that working out for you?"

"Heartburn is better, but I'm still in a lot of pain, and I get really tired really easily."

"I see."

He flipped through the chart some more and adjusted his glasses. He told me to have a seat on the exam table as he began the routine. He checked my eyes, ears, nose, mouth, neck, knees, heart and lungs. His thick hands rested in places I didn't normally let strangers touch, but I reminded myself that this was for my health and to help make me better.

"Well everything sounds and looks good in those areas. You say you're still feeling a lot of pain and fatigue? And you say you're taking the medications as prescribed?" He didn't seem to believe me.

"Yes," I said, this time with decisive certainty.

He took my arms and studied them closely, the way Papi had attempted to do earlier without even knowing what he was looking for. He asked me to make a fist. I did to the best of my ability, but my hands would not close entirely. He asked me to lift my arms up as high as I could for as long as I could. I tried. But after a few moments, they fell limply to my side. These trials and errors did not please Papi, who grunted and shook his head side to side. I turned to look away from his disgust only to find Mami almost in tears. I knew they shouldn't have come. I hated making Mami cry. I still blamed myself for what was happening to me and I hadn't understood or accepted yet that this disease wasn't my fault. The guilt of all the lies I had told them recently to cover up that I had quit my job, along with my ailing body, festered and turned inside my stomach.

Papi would not be defeated. He walked up to Dr. Malloy and said, "Okay, doctor, so what can you do for her? What is going to make her better? When is she going to get better? The medicine you're giving her isn't working. What are we going to do to fix this?" He asked each question without pause, staring the doctor down, demanding that he prove himself.

Papi, a man who because of his skin color and broken English had always had to prove himself to others, would accept nothing less from this colored man either. Dr. Malloy would have to earn Papi's trust and respect.

"Well, sir," the doctor began mildly, "you have to understand that scleroderma is a chronic, auto-immune disease that, at this point in time, has no known direct cause and no cure."

I began to let the hum of the AC fill my ears. I felt the doctor's voice trail off. I'd heard his speech at least twice before and had read all the facts about it on the internet at least a hundred times when I was still trying to convince myself that it was all a bad dream. My eyes began to glaze over and I daydreamed about the cute male nurse. I pictured his buff arms, his round ass and his gorgeous smile.

Then, I felt guilty about fantasizing about him since I had a boyfriend who loved me and had been taking care of me financially and emotionally for the last few months. I shook off my fantasy and thought about what I was going to eat for lunch instead. Mami was in town, so that meant I could ask for anything I wanted. I imagined a pot of arroz con pollo and plátanos fritos. My mouth watered and I felt warm inside.

Mami put her hand on my shoulder as if sensing that I wasn't fully in the room, and I came back to reality. She looked like she was trying hard to hold back the tears. Shit, I thought, if she cries, I'm going to cry. Please don't cry. I smiled at her and squeezed her hand despite the pain it caused in my knuckles. She didn't cry. I wondered what the hell the doctor had said. Shit, I should have been listening.

"Okay. So we're going to start you on methylprednisolone, increase the dosage of Naproxen to 400 mg a day instead of 200 mg and continue on the Protonix for the heartburn."

I was shaken by all the complex names of prescriptions he'd just rattled off and was still worried about what he'd said to Mami to make her want to cry. I hated this doctor. He had no right to shove Mami and Papi out of the denial phase just yet. That was my job, not his. Couldn't he see that they were too fragile? Didn't he understand that they had to believe that something, anything could still be done to fix this, cure me, reverse the damage? I hated him for breaking them, just as much as I hated scleroderma for breaking me. I hopped off the table, thanked him and walked out. My parents scurried after me, waving the prescriptions in the air.

"We should go next door to the pharmacy and fill these right away," said Papi.

"Fine. But we should get something to eat soon. I'm hungry and I'm getting a headache." I was too frustrated and angry to focus on the implications of what filling this prescription meant. I was ready to leave that office and never return.

When I walked into the Walgreens pharmacy directly across the street from the doctor's office, the fluorescent lights clouded my vision. The aisles and aisles of shelves stacked with over the counter remedies, pills, bandages, creams and concoctions overwhelmed my senses. It smelled of rubbing alcohol and bleach like the doctor's office from before, but there was also the floral scent of lavender from gift candles and detergent hovering around every corner. I took the long walk back to the actual pharmacy counter and wondered why the one thing patients actually came here for was located at the very back of the store. Why was it necessary to traverse all the aisles of cosmetics and housewares before tending to one's actual medicinal needs? The walk made me short of breath. Mami and Papi hurried behind me, but I was trying to take care of this without their intervention or help. I was still trying to keep my dirty little secret of being uninsured and practically unemployed.

When I arrived at the counter, I handed the pharmacist the prescriptions and my insurance card. He took it and asked me to wait in the cubicle-sized space next to the counter. I sat down as Mami and Papi approached. Mami placed her hand on my shoulder and looked at me concerned.

"¿Qué pasó?" She sat next to me and placed her other warm hand on top of mine.

"Nada. I'm just waiting for the pharmacist to get the prescription."

My nerves and my senses were on overdrive. Any moment now, I knew I would burst into tears. I knew the pharmacist was calling my insurance and finding out that I was no longer covered. I knew that at any moment I would have to reveal the truth. I felt my stomach in my throat. The fluorescent lights buzzed, and I felt their glare trembling in my periphery. I tried to focus on the flu shot poster on the adjacent wall. Mami continued to pat my hands. She knew I wasn't well, mothers always know, but she didn't know why. The pharmacist called my name. I got up, one vertebra at a time, and approached the counter clutching my purse.

"We called your insurance company but they say you aren't covered with them anymore," the pharmacist began. "Do you have any other form of coverage?"

Papi, who had been standing right behind me, heard everything. He squeezed in front of me and addressed the pharmacist.

"What do you mean she has no insurance? We just saw the doctor. Check again. Check it again."

My face flushed red. I had forced Papi to try and defend me based on a lie. This had all gone too far. I sighed and moved up next to Papi at the counter. I clutched my purse hoping to find the strength to tell him the truth.

"Papi, no, it's okay." I turned to look at the pharmacist. "I don't have insurance. It's okay. I'll just self-pay today. Thank you."

Mami and Papi said nothing. I turned to face Papi and blurted out the truth.

"I don't have insurance, Papi. I quit my job six months ago y ya no tengo seguro. Pero está bien. I'll be fine. I have the money to pay for it."

It was another lie. But at least, I believed, that one wouldn't hurt as much. They stared at me and at each other, waiting for more of an explanation. I didn't have one for them. I could not make them understand in that moment that making art was more important than making money. They were immigrants who came from nothing to make something of their lives and mine. I could not possibly make them understand that I was okay with having less if it meant being emotionally fulfilled. As soon as the pharmacist called again, I handed my debit card and hoped that it wouldn't be declined. The payment went through. I signed the receipt, he handed me the plastic bag with the orange pill bottles inside and gave me some instructions. I rushed out of the store with Mami and Papi scurrying behind me. Outside, I found an empty bus stop bench and sat down. Mami and Papi sat down next to me. Papi was the first to speak.

"¿Pero, por qué? ¿Por qué?" He shook his head, clenching his hat in his hands. He wanted to know why I hadn't told them. He wanted to know if he had treated me so badly in life that I couldn't trust him to tell him the truth. Why didn't I believe that they would understand? He wanted to know what he had done to deserve this deception? "¡Dime!"

But I didn't have an answer. All I had were hot tears and a belly full of regret and fear. I swallowed and tried to give them an answer because I was the cause of their pain. And the guilt I felt sat on my chest like a sack full of rice that stifled my breath.

"Because, because I didn't know how to tell you. Because I didn't want to disappoint you. It was such a good job and ya'll were so proud of me I didn't want you and Mami to have to keep worrying about me. You already have enough to worry about."

In that moment, I realized that in an effort to keep them from being disappointed in me, I had done something worse: I had made them disappointed in themselves. My heart burned. My head pounded. The sack on my chest grew heavier and made me sob.

"Ay, Yamina. No te pongas así. Calm down." Mami handed me a tissue.

As I grabbed it, she took hold of my hand. Her hand felt warm and soft like fresh-baked bread. I didn't want to let go. She sighed and nestled her head in my shoulder. The wind blew and sent a wave of her perfume into my nostrils. I could breathe again. Papi shifted on the bench, taking his hat on and off, wiping his brow, shaking his head in disbelief.

"It doesn't matter what we go through. We are here for you. And you need to trust us. With everything. It's the only way we can help you." Papi stomped his left foot on the pavement, kicked some dirt, like an angry kid throwing a tantrum, and wiped away the unwanted tears and sweat from his rugged but wrinkle-free, dark face.

"I know, Papi, and I'm sorry."

Mami put her arm around me, and I felt her heavy breathing against my neck. It made me shiver, and she pulled me in even closer.

"Ay, Yamina, ¿qué vamos a hacer contigo?"

Mami was trying to hold back the tears but she'd never been any good at that. I stroked her hair to try and put her at ease.

"Yo sé, Mami. I know. I'm too independent and I just didn't want to give you another reason to worry about me." That was partly the truth, but Mami knew me well enough to know that it was not the whole truth.

"No, tú no quieres que te controlen. Yo te conozco." She sat up and gave me the all-knowing side-eye and pursed-lip stare that only mothers have perfected. I conceded.

"Well, yes, that too. I don't like to be controlled, you're right. I wanted to do this on my own. I thought I could do this. But really, I also just didn't want you to be disappointed in me." I hugged her again.

She sucked her teeth and sighed, repeating, "Ay, Yamina, ay, Yamina, qué vamos a hacer contigo."

SKIN SCORE

-3-

IN THE FIFTH GRADE, I dated a boy named Gary. He was the most popular and athletic boy in our class. Gary played football, basketball and tetherball like a pro. He had pearly white teeth and dimples that made all the girls giggle when he smiled. He always told the funniest "yo momma" jokes. Although I didn't really understand what being boyfriend and girlfriend meant at our age, I figured that if I was his girlfriend, it would mean that I could be popular too. I was the new girl that year, and most of the other kids thought I was "weird" because I was "mixed" with "good hair" and could speak Spanish. Being Gary's girlfriend would help me fit in and be liked by everyone else.

Everything went well for a few weeks. We held hands under the table at lunch, played together at recess and passed notes in class. But the longer we were boyfriend and girlfriend, the more afraid I was that Mami and Papi would find out. I wasn't allowed to have boyfriends at that age and I didn't want to get in trouble if they somehow figured it out. I told Gary I couldn't be his girlfriend anymore. That's when the bullying started. I don't know if it was because I bruised his ego or if it was his pre-pubescent childish way of handling rejection, but I became his target. He managed to turn almost the entire fifth grade class against me.

He nicknamed me, "It," and told all the other fifth graders to refuse to sit next to me in class or at lunch. They made a pact that if I tried to talk to them or if I had to read aloud in class or present a project, they would cover their ears and close their eyes so they wouldn't have to listen to or look at me. When I passed a group of them in the hallway, they would point, laugh and chant, "It, It, It." If I happened to brush by one of their desks, or bump into one of them, they acted like I had contaminated them with a terrible disease and they wiped themselves down or washed their hands. I had no friends and no one to ask for help. I tried to tell Ms. Bell, our teacher, but Gary was the teacher's pet. She told me she just couldn't believe he would do such a thing. She spoke to him privately, but he never got in trouble.

During this time, I learned to depend on myself. I built a wall around my heart, and even when some of the kids tried to be nice to me, I treated them with indifference. I did not want or need friends. Instead, I borrowed books from the library and let the characters in the stories keep me company. I enjoyed losing myself in such novels as *The Giver* and *Harriet the Spy*, and my best friend became Laura from a book called *And This Is Laura*. It was one of my favorite books because it was about a girl who was intuitive and could tell the future. She saved lives and helped people despite being ostracized because no one believed she had special gifts. I liked characters like Harriet, Laura and Jonas because they were different and exceptional, the way I had hoped to be.

I retreated into the worlds created by books and I started to create new worlds in poems and stories I wrote about the apocalypse, the end of holidays and travelling back and forth through time. I used words to create supporting characters that loved the main character, me, and I fell in love with books and characters that could never reject me or make me feel bad. I used the stories I read to block out the bullies. I used the words I wrote to build me up and stifle my grief. I never told my parents about the bullying and I never spoke about it to anyone. I convinced myself I was stronger and better than all those immature kids because I knew I was exceptional. One day, they would all see it.

The bullying continued through middle school, and every time I walked past Gary and his friends, they would chant, "It, It, It." I'd hold my head up high and repeat to myself, "Sticks and stones may break my bones, but your words will never hurt me."

-2-

My school drama classes taught me how to handle rejection. I loved performing in plays and auditioning for them helped me learn how to accept the word "no."

I loved theatre and performance, and during those adolescent years, I used acting and drama to escape my own realities and teen angst. I immersed myself in every supporting and minor role I was given and always made sure to be the most memorable character on stage. I hissed and crawled along the stage when I played the part of Gollum in *The Hobbit*. I practiced my sultry walk and southern accent when I played a sassy secretary in the play *Machinal*. I was told by my teachers and classmates that I was talented. I believed them because I kept getting cast in various roles but never the lead role. The fact of the matter was, my white theatre teacher, Mrs. Bachmann only chose what me and the other black theatre kids in class called "pre-emancipation" plays. These were plays that were written before the Civil Rights Movement or, God forbid, before the end of slavery. "Classic plays" like *The Importance of Being Earnest*, *Our Town* and *Death of A Salesman,* where people of color didn't exist, or worse, could only be cast as the help, the janitor, the busboy or the nanny. Based on traditional casting methods, it was clear our teachers didn't believe in colorblind casting, but we didn't let their outright biases stop us.

My classmates and I always auditioned for *all* the roles, no matter what. We memorized our one-minute audition monologues and came prepared and on time to callbacks. Yet, to everyone else's surprise (not ours), our names were never listed for the leading roles. Even though our teachers always assured us that we were some of the most talented students in the class, they'd always say we didn't "fit the part."

During the spring semester of my junior year, I summoned up the courage to confront Mrs. Bachmann about what I felt was unfair and discriminatory. She was the head of the department and was usually in charge of selecting the plays for the season. I knew there was strength in numbers, so I asked my friends to join me when I spoke to her. I figured she couldn't possibly deny ALL of us what we were asking for and she would have to consider our plea carefully.

We approached her one afternoon before rehearsal for our current show, *Splendor in the Grass*, a play set in the 1960s about a teenage couple in the Midwest. In this show, though I had auditioned for the lead, I was given the role of the teacher. I was in one scene and only had five lines.

When I walked into the black box that afternoon, Mrs. Bachmann was sitting center stage in her navy blue director's chair, legs crossed, flipping her hair with one hand, holding a number two pencil in the other and scratching notes into the black binder on her lap. We walked up to her assertively and I asked: "Would you consider directing an all-black play? We have the actors, the sets are simple and the English teachers would love it!"

She raised her head slowly from the script and furrowed her perfectly arched eyebrows.

I continued, "We could totally do it! It could even be like in February for Black History Month or something. It would be great! It would be a lot of fun for us!"

She took a deep breath and cocked her head to the side, her blond hair falling into her eyes.

"Maybe. But like what kind of play are you thinking?"

I jumped right in because I was prepared for this question. "We could do a classic like *Fences* or *A Raisin in the Sun*. Something we could invite all the English classes to." I was practically hopping up and down at this point, and my classmates were egging me on saying "Yes, yeah" and "Mmmhmm."

Mrs. Bachmann closed her black notebook, stuck the number two pencil behind her ear, looked at the four of us, smiled wide with her bright red lips, tossed her hair to the side and said quite plainly, "But, *Jaaasminne*, how would that make the other students feel?"

My body stiffened. The way she had said my name made me feel dirty. I didn't care how it would make the other students feel because I had been feeling that way for years. I decided I was done trying to prove myself to her or anyone else. If she didn't want me to have a lead role on stage, that was her loss. I would find my own way to do theatre.

Later that spring semester, I wrote up and gave Mrs. Bachmann a proposal to direct a play the following year. The rest of the teachers in the theatre department thought it would be a great idea to have a student-directed show and agreed that I was the most capable, talented and responsible student to do it.

On my senior year I became the first student to select and direct her own show. I made sure to choose a contemporary play, *The Shadowbox,* and to cast as many students of color as I could. The play and the casting were groundbreaking for our campus. Our cast was later featured in a two-page spread in the yearbook. I could tell Mrs. Bachmann didn't like all the attention I received for it. While I was directing the show, she avoided me in the hallways and treated me coldly in class. Because everyone else around school, including the principal, applauded my work, Mrs. Bachmann never did say my name that way again.

-1-

I was called several nicknames by my parents growing up: Jas, Yamina, Ya and Morusa. Morusa is what Mami used to call me all the time. Whenever she said it, she would grab my nose between her index and middle finger and squeeze really hard until I screamed or started to cry. Then she would laugh and give me a big hug.

One Thanksgiving holiday during college, I invited Mami to have a pedicure. She had been complaining about feeling tired and sloppy, so I decided to treat her to a spa day. After our appointment, while in the car at a stoplight, she looked at me, grabbed my nose and said, "Gracias, mi Morusa, esto era lo que necesitaba. Me siento mejor."

I wiggled my face out of her grasp and yelled, "Ma! Why do you do that? And what does "morusa" even mean?"

She laughed and shook her head. "¿Ay, Yamina, para qué quieres saber?" She looked carefully at her nails to make sure she hadn't messed them up by pinching my nose.

"I don't know. You've just always called me that, and I've never known what it meant. Is it because I have a large nose?"

She laughed even harder now and shook her head some more. "Bueno, you know, when you see a chicken or a rooster and that top part on their head is all nappy-headed and tangled and wild, sabes, that part is called the morusa." She motioned towards her widow's peak and made her fingers stand straight up on her forehead.

My face fell in shock.

"Ma! You mean it has nothing to do with my nose?"

"No, ¿por qué? Why would you think that?"

"Because you always grabbed my nose when you said it!"

She laughed and shook her head. "No. It's because your hair was always wild, no matter how much I combed and brushed it. Eres una morusa."

"Wow. Gracias, Ma. Thanks for referring to me as a nappy-headed chicken my whole life." I couldn't help but laugh.

"Ay, you know it's all out of love." And when she touched my frizzy hair, it sent goose bumps all over my arms and down my spine.

-2-

I dated a Sikh man in college. His name was Guru. We were both actors. We had met during rehearsals for a show my freshman year. For two years, we had a relationship that we both knew was not long-term. I was not a Sikh nor an Indian. He was not a Latino nor a Catholic. We were both only in our early twenties, and marriage was not even in our vocabulary. But we did have a good time when we were together. We drank, smoked out, went to cast parties after shows and generally had a good time.

I loved it when he let me braid his floor-length, black, silky hair and wrap it up in his turban. I studied the way our skin was almost the same shade of brown, but mine had a hint of olive and his a hint of red. I cringed at the way he doused everything in hot sauce because, when he kissed me, I could taste it. I liked the way he called me "Mina," when I answered his calls. Mina, short for Yamina, what he heard Mami call me over the phone once. I liked it because he was the only person to take my Spanish name and make it his own. Every waking moment that we were not in class or in rehearsal, Guru and I cuddled up on a couch or a bed and listened to electric guitars and drums. He introduced me to alternative indie bands, such as Mars Volta, the Postal Service and the White Stripes. Music helped us live in the moment of who we were and not who our families wanted us to be. Whether we studied theatre or law, engineering or creative writing, didn't matter when we were together. We had no expectations of who we would become or what our relationship should mean. We only cared about being together and talking about books, music, acting and movies.

Although we rarely went out on real dates, because we were college students and didn't have the money for that kind of thing, he did invite me once to his sister's one-year wedding anniversary celebration. We were at his apartment eating our usual fare of pizza and ice cream for dinner when he brought up the party.

"This party is going to be huge. Almost as big as a wedding. My sister's so crazy. They rented a venue, hired caterers and ordered two cakes. There'll even be a DJ."

"Wow, that is pretty intense. For a wedding anniversary?"

"Yeah. Indian folks do it big, ya know."

"Yeah, I can see that. So you actually think it's okay if I come with you?"

"Well, sort of. They need a bartender. And I suggested you. They've already spent so much money on the liquor, but the venue isn't providing a bartender."

"Dude, I've never bartended. I wouldn't know what to do!"

"Don't worry about it. They're going to ask for simple stuff like rum and coke or beer."

"I don't know. I wouldn't want to mess this up."

"It's okay. Just do it. And you'll get tips. And we can hang out afterwards."

"I guess so. But only 'cause I'm getting tips."

He hugged me and kissed me on the cheek.

I'd never met his parents, and he had never met mine. I had met his sister before. She was down-to-earth and didn't really care about his love life. For this occasion, however, I had to meet and talk to his mom. I didn't know what he had told her about me, but I knew it would probably be an awkward exchange.

As a female, he told me that I needed to be appropriately dressed for a Sikh party.

"Okay, so what does that mean?"

"We gotta go to my sister's house so you can borrow one of her saris."

"Oh. That sounds like fun. They're all so pretty. I'm actually really excited about this."

"Good."

The weekend before the party, I went to his sister's, rummaged through her closet and picked out a red and black floral number with silver beading along the sleeves. The sari exposed my midriff and hung soft and silky around my shoulders. It cascaded down my back and dragged on the floor behind me when I walked. It looked great on me. I was excited to make a few bucks, and it was fun to wear something different and be immersed in his culture for once.

When I arrived at the venue dressed in my borrowed sari, ready to work, Guru introduced me to his mom, as his friend, the bartender. I was not offended. I knew no one needed to know about us. I didn't want him to have to explain anything to his mom or make this anymore awkward than what it had to be.

I smiled and said, "Hello, my name is Jasminne."

His mother, wearing a teal and blue sari with sequins and a pattern more intricate and elaborate than the one I wore, shook my hand and looked me up and down. She did not smile. She moved her head side to side like a dashboard doll, her charcoal-colored hair sat like a braided crown on her head.

"Oh, you dress like an Indian and you have Indian name," she said, "but you, you are not Indian."

She scanned my body again, her eyes dancing to the rhythm of the bhangra music in the background. Guru laughed. My sari slipped off my shoulder and I tried to smile. I knew her directness was a cultural thing. The older women in my family were exactly the same: stubborn, straightforward and strong. I realized then that Latinas and Sikh women weren't so different, after all. I had grown up around comments like these my whole life, but what stung me was my boyfriend's laughter. I didn't expect him to come to my defense, because I knew his mom didn't know about us. But the fact that he laughed and never bothered to apologize for his mom's comment at any point during the night reminded me that I was an outsider in his world and that there was no future to the relationship.

I thanked his mom for allowing me to bartend. He placed his hand between her shoulder blades to nudge her forward. She lifted her sari off the floor, shook her head and they walked away.

I watched him escort her to the ballroom. They blurred beneath the strobe lights. Her sequined sari shimmered beneath the disco ball and broke into a thousand tiny rainbows on the floor. I fumbled with the borrowed fabric that hung awkwardly off my shoulder and tried to put it back in its place.

-3-

My first full-time job while attending graduate school was as a teaching assistant in an elementary school. I worked with second-through fifth-grade students in small groups, made copies, decorated bulletin boards, filed paperwork and was also on breakfast and lunch duty in the cafeteria. It was tedious work, but it was only for a year and I needed classroom experience if I expected to get a teaching job after graduate school.

During the first faculty meeting of the year, the teachers had to go around and introduce ourselves. Most of the teachers, like most of the students at this school, were Latino. Almost everyone was bilingual and had a Spanish last name. In any given classroom, there could be three students named José; four, María; and three, Miguel. The teachers and teaching assistants had such surnames as Hernández, González, Uriaga and Montemayor. They were all from places like Guatemala, El Salvador and Mexico. As far as I could tell, there were only three racially black people on faculty or staff: Mrs. Jones, the middle-aged ready-to-retire special education teacher who changed her weave as often as her outfits; Anthony Moore, a young black man who I learned later had a kid on the way and needed the teaching assistant job for the health insurance; and me, a naïve graduate student entering the professional world for the first time. As I made the rounds to introduce myself, I began with Mrs. Jones. She seemed the most approachable, and we hit it off right away. She told me to come sit next to her once I was done introducing myself to everyone. I made my way around the room, shaking hands and smiling. With the bilingual teachers, I even said, "¿Cómo estás?" and "Mucho gusto." Some of them would squint their eyes, trying to understand where I was from. Once I explained that my family was from the Dominican Republic, they would nod and say, "Ahhh," as if I had just revealed some secret to the universe.

One of the last people I introduced myself to was the nurse.

"Hello. I'm Jasminne. Jasminne Rosario. ¿Cómo estás?"

The nurse, a four-foot tall Mexican woman with dark black hair and thick glasses, reached for my hand, grabbed it, squeezed it hard, pulled me in towards her and asked me again in Spanish what my name was.

"Jasminne Rosario, soy la Señorita Rosario."

She shook her head as if she didn't understand. She continued to grip my hand and wouldn't let it go. "¿Rosario? Your last name is Rosario?"

"Yes. Rosario is my last name. Jasminne is my first name."

She shook her head in what was either disgust or disbelief, I couldn't tell which, and finally let my hand go.

"In Mexico, Rosario is a common name. Es un nombre para la criada. Have you seen telenovelas? There is always a maid named Rosario."

"Yes, I know. Pero yo soy dominicana. And in the Dominican Republic, Rosario, or del Rosario as it was originally, is a last name. It's my family's name with a long legacy of educators and artists." I felt proud that I knew the history of my name and could enlighten her.

"Hmmm," she said, staring me up and down in a very judgemental, Latina grandma kind of way. She nodded, pursed her lips and said nothing else.

I walked away from her and made eye contact with Mrs. Jones who was sitting next to Anthony. She waved me over, and I found a seat in the back of the room next to her.

"How's it going?" she asked as she took off her glasses and wiped them with a Kleenex.

"It's going to be a long year," I said.

She nodded and placed her hand on my shoulder.

"I know, girl. I know."

-1, 2, 3-

"So where did you hear of this doctor again?" asked Papi as he stared into a magazine while we waited in the exam room for the doctor to arrive.

After Mami and Papi had accompanied me to my rheumatologist appointment, Dr. Malloy had refused to change any of my medications despite their ineffectiveness and would only see me every six months. I knew my symptoms were worsening and I needed better treatment. I had done some research and found that Houston actually had one of the top scleroderma research centers in the country.

"Well, I found out about a Dr. Hayes online, but she's busy until next year. So her nurse recommended this doctor."

"Okay, and what makes these doctors so good?" Always the skeptic, Papi wanted facts, charts and graphs to prove my claims.

"Well, I don't really know, Papi. But other patients say they're some of the best in the country. And this is a research facility, so they do studies here."

"Oh. Studies, really?" Papi had a soft spot for school, education and the never-ending pursuit of knowledge and truth. "Can they put you in a study? Can they test us too and see what is causing all this?"

"Well, I don't know, Papi. But we can ask."

"Good, good. That's good. I like this place."

"I'm glad you approve," I said sarcastically.

He glared at me above his reading glasses and returned to his magazine. My feet dangled from the exam table like a child in a high chair.

"¿Cuánto se van a tardar?" asked Mami impatiently. She gripped her purse and bit her lip anxiously.

"It hasn't really been that long, Mami."

"But you have to get back to work, don't you?"

"Yes, but it's fine." We all knew she wasn't worried about me getting back to work on time, she was just worried about me.

A few minutes later a middle-aged, yet fairly attractive, dark-haired man in a white lab coat and black Gucci glasses walked into the room.

"Good morning! I am Dr. Hassan," he said cheerfully and shook Papi's hand, then Mami's and finally mine. "So, how are you today?" He smiled and spoke directly to me now.

As much as I had grown to hate those words coming from anyone lately, I couldn't help but feel like a box of warm cookies every time he smiled.

"I'm okay," I said shortly, hoping there wouldn't be too much small talk.

"So, these are your parents, yes?"

"Yes."

"Good. Well then, tell me about yourself. What brings you here today?"

My feet dangled. I stared at the floor. I clutched the sides of the cold, plastic bed. The paper sheet beneath me rattled and sounded loud in the small room.

"Well, I was diagnosed with scleroderma last November and . . . "

I went on to tell him my whole medical history as best I could remember it. I stuck to the facts and I didn't allow myself to get emotional because I needed him to know that I was strong. I needed him to know that I was ready to do whatever it took to beat this thing.

I ended by saying, "And I'm here because I didn't like my other doctors and I want to know what kind of scleroderma I have. Is it limited, diffuse, systemic or what?" I took a deep breath and looked him straight in the eye. I would not leave without a better treatment plan.

"Well, let's get started. After I'm done with the exam, I'll tell you what kind of scleroderma you have." He motioned to my par-

ents, "Let's all step outside while you change into a gown, and we'll
be right back."

He led my parents out of the room and I changed. After a few
minutes everyone returned, including a resident. Dr. Hassan introduced him.

"This is Dr. Berg. He is a student here at the medical school. He
will be helping me and observing the examination today." I shook
Dr. Berg's hand and I suddenly felt like a circus freak, ready to be
gawked at, poked and prodded by onlookers. My feet were dangling
off the bed again and I adjusted the gown.

"You're a little cold?" Dr. Hassan pointed at my toes. They were
blue, and so were my fingertips.

"Yeah, just a little." I laughed nervously. I didn't know what else
to do.

"Cold and nervous, I bet," he said, smiling again.

"Yes. Both, I guess."

He went to the sink and washed his hands with warm water. This
was the first time any doctor had thought to be so considerate of my
condition. He didn't want to touch me with cold hands. Some of my
apprehension and fear began to fade. Dr. Hassan started the examination by squeezing the skin on my fingers and toes. He pinched the
top of my left foot and said the number, three, and Dr. Berg wrote it
down. He pinched the top of my right foot, my shins, my thighs, my
stomach, my chest, my arms, the back of both my hands, my chin
and underneath my eye. After each pinch he said a number between
one and three.

When he was done, I asked him, "What was all that?"

"That is called a skin score. Patients can score from a zero to a
three. Zero means you have no involvement, or that the skin is not
affected. One indicates mild involvement, two is moderate and three
is severe. The higher the number, the more skin involvement you
have in that area."

"Oh. So how much skin involvement do I have overall?"

"Let's see." He read over the chart and added the numbers in his
head. "You have a skin score of 32."

"Oh. And is that really bad?"

"Well, it does show significant skin involvement, but at your stage in the disease and with the limited treatment you've had, it could be worse."

Dr. Hassan finished the rest of my exam by listening to my heart and my lungs. He then explained that I had limited scleroderma with CREST. CREST was a form of systemic sclerosis, which was characterized by: calcinosis (calcium deposits), usually in the fingers; Raynaud's phenomenon; loss of muscle control of the esophagus, which caused difficulty swallowing; sclerodactyly, a tapering deformity of the bones in the fingers; and telangiectasia, small red spots on the skin of the fingers, face or inside of the mouth. Based on my own research and because I had been living with all the symptoms he described almost too a T, I believed him.

"So what's next?"

"Well, we'll need to treat you aggressively if we don't want your symptoms to worsen or to spread to your internal organs. There is the possibility that you could get scarring in the lungs or have kidney or heart involvement. I am going to schedule a round of tests, including an echo and a pulmonary function test to check your lung capacity. It doesn't sound like you have lung involvement yet, but we won't be sure until we run these tests."

"Okay, and what about medication?"

"Well, there are a number of experimental medications that can help slow the progression of the disease and possibly even reverse it. But as you know, there is no cure."

"Doctor, what causes scleroderma?" Papi interrupted because he was ready for some kind of an answer.

"Well, sir, we do not know. It is a combination of genetic and environmental factors. We know stress can trigger the symptoms, but we don't know yet what the specific cause of the disease is or who is more likely to develop it."

"So, it's genetic?" It was clear that Papi had only heard a part of what Dr. Hassan said.

"Based on some of the research we've done, we believe there is a genetic component, yes, but that is not the only factor."

"Okay, okay. But it's possible it came from me or her mother?"

"I cannot tell you that for sure, sir."

Papi was looking for someone or something to blame. Dr. Hassan's vague answers were not good enough, but it was all he was going to get today.

I interrupted Papi's interrogation because I was cold and ready to get out of the hospital gown.

"Thank you, Dr. Hassan, for all your help. I look forward to starting the new medications." I reached out to shake his hand. He shook mine and handed me my prescriptions. "Fill and start these as soon as possible. Go downstairs and get the bloodwork done today. The nurse will call you to set up the pulmonary function test and the echo."

My parents thanked the doctor and left the room so I could get dressed. I sat on the exam table for a moment and stared at my blue fingers. I pinched the skin of my left forearm. It was difficult to pull up. It was scaly and dark like the flesh of an alligator, and no one could tell me why. I remembered reading in a self-help book that the illnesses our bodies carried were a manifestation of our thoughts and our subconscious. If this was true, then was the leathery snakeskin layer of dermis that now coated most of my arms, chest, neck and legs a response to years of the mishandled trauma and grief I had buried to prove to the world and myself that I was just as good, if not better, than everyone else? Was scleroderma my body's way of keeping score of all the insults, racial slurs, bullying and micro-aggressions I had chosen to repress? And if it took years of painful experiences and rejection for my skin to form this shield and scleroderma to manifest, how long would it take and what would it take to shed this thickened skin and start anew?

POET'S JASMIN(N)E

NOW LUPE CALLS ME AMO, but our romance didn't begin as a romance or even a friendship for that matter. Lupe and I met when were both cast in a play at a community theater and I was still learning how to master the art of sincere kindness and humility. I was/am sarcastic and grumpy by nature. I had been told that was a trait I should try to work on, but at the time I didn't see anything wrong with it. He, on the other hand, was "Mr. Happy Center of Attention." I hated his jovial and gregarious nature. I didn't understand how or why someone could be so happy all the time. I believed that life was serious. Theatre was serious. Why wasn't he serious? His joy irritated me. He found my bitterness obnoxious and perplexing. I thought he was too old to act so childish. He thought I was too young to be so jaded.

We eventually warmed up to each other when we realized we were the best actors in the cast. As we began to talk sparingly backstage, wondering how and why we ended up in such a terrible play, I started to develop a crush on him. He was a funny and attractive Latino who spoke Spanish, had a real job and, best of all, a perfect smile with dimples. He was short, but so was I. That was okay because I had always found it awkward when I'd dated tall guys. His skin was olive, like mine, but more Indio, and his thick black hair assured me that he'd never go bald. His broad back, thick calves and square frame assured me his body was built for hard work and strong hugs. Suddenly, I wanted him to notice me, but being that sarcasm was my default, my flirting and advances toward him came in the form of crude jokes at his expense. One day he came into rehearsal in his usual jovial mood, threw his hands up in the air, grinned and said, "Good evening, everyone! How's everybody doing tonight?" I smiled coyly and said, "Fine, until you got here." He shrugged, rolled his eyes and completely dismissed me by walking to the other side of the room. I was hurt that he didn't retort something just as insulting back. Did he not know how to flirt? Needless to say, he didn't like that approach. For a few days, every time I met him with sarcasm, he continued to ignore me, the young cynic with a bad sense of humor. After a few days of this, my confidence began to wane. I wasn't sure I could ever get him to notice me, much less like me or go out with me. But I was determined to try, so I changed my approach.

Instead of poking fun at him, I decided to make jokes about the other actors on stage while we waited for our cues to enter. This made him laugh, and he joined in on the fun. We danced the robot when one of the actors who spoke in a monotone voice and performed his lines mechanically time and time again. We crudely mimicked the choreographer with a broken foot who tried to show a rhythm-less cast how to dance. And we imitated the director combing his hair side to side despite the fact that he was practically bald. After a few days of this, I could tell he was warming up to me.

My real infatuation began when I attended a poetry reading he invited the entire cast to. Only two of us actually went, and we sat in the front row. When Lupe read his poetry, my schoolgirl crush began to evolve into something deeper. This man could act, dance AND write poetry! My stomach fluttered, my eyes glistened. For the first time I saw his bright smile and dimples and, instead of rolling my eyes, I smiled back, even though he wasn't even looking at me.

After he got off stage, he made the rounds and said hello to all his friends while I stood back, hoping he'd acknowledge that I had come. But he didn't. He had said hello to everyone but me. Before I could get his attention, he left to go to a samba party.

That night, tired of playing games, I sent him a text message: "So, do you flirt with all the girls, or just me?"

I waited by my phone for over an hour. He didn't respond. It was well past two in the morning, so I resigned myself to being ignored and went to bed. An hour later my phone buzzed. I rolled over and looked at the glowing screen: "You know you want this." I sat up in bed amused and slightly upset. I didn't know if he was serious or if he was just joking. I didn't know how to respond. I sent the text to my sister, but she was no help. All she texted back was: "Lol. Haha." I decided it was best to not respond, to keep him guessing. I didn't want to play games and was too tired to craft a flirty "come hither" response. The next morning, I decided I didn't want to waste any more time. I was determined to be straightforward and honest. He was going to know that I was interested in him, and he would have to decide right then and there if he was interested in me too. I grabbed my phone and sent him a message: "So, do you like me or not?" It was the adult and modern-day version of the hand scribbled note: Do you like me? Circle YES or NO.

I waited in bed with phone in hand, anxious for a response. The screen glowed. "Maybe." I threw my phone across the bed. I screamed into a pillow. Who the hell was this man? Why was he being so evasive? I really didn't have time for these games. I reached for the phone again and replied: "What do you mean 'maybe'?" It buzzed right back: "Depends, I'd have to take you out first." Finally, I thought, a real answer. I beamed. He was actually asking me out on a date. A few messages later, we set a time to meet up for lunch.

❧   ❧   ❧

About a year and half into our relationship, shortly after I was diagnosed and was in and out of bouts of depression and self-loathing, I decided to give Lupe a way out of our relationship. We were lying in bed, not saying much, just enjoying each other's warmth.

"Honey, do you think I'm still beautiful?"

"Of course, you are," he answered, brushing the hair out of my eyes. He kissed me on the cheek.

I shoved my face into his ribcage. I didn't feel good enough for him then. I thought for sure that my illness would hold him back from his dreams, his career, his future family life. I felt that if I was sick, it was because I had done something wrong in life. Therefore, I definitely didn't deserve this man or his love. I was ready to let him go if it meant that he would have a happier life.

"I want you to know that if you want to leave, now or any time in the future, I won't blame you. I'll understand." I said this to the pillow, because I knew I'd start to cry if I looked at him.

He squeezed me tighter. "Where would I go?"

"I don't know. You could find some sweet Mexican hottie who can cook and clean and iron your shirts and make fresh tortillas and have your babies."

"What if I want you to have my babies?"

"But this illness, this disease, it might get worse. What if it gets worse? What if I can't have your babies? You don't have to stay. I won't blame you. When we met, I wasn't sick. This isn't what you signed up for." I moved in closer and shoved my head into the space between his shoulder and his neck. He smelled like fresh linen and sweat. I closed my eyes and nuzzled my nose into his T-shirt. I was still too afraid to look at him.

"Babe, I'm not going anywhere." He pulled my chin up and smiled. "You ain't getting rid of me that easily." I was not enough for him. He deserved better. I needed him to see that.

"But, seriously. What if I lose my fingers, or I end up on an oxygen tank, or in a wheelchair or . . . "

He pulled me close and the rest of my words sank into his chest.

"Amo. I love you, hoy y siempre. That's not going to change, no matter what your fingers look like, or what machines you have to drag around."

Because I believed him and because I could tell he had made up his mind, all I could say was, "I love you too."

"Just promise me one thing." He picked my chin up with his right hand and wrapped one of my curls around his fingers.

"What?"

"Promise me that before you lose those pretty little fingers, you'll learn how to make menudo and frijoles a la charra."

"You mean habichuelas guisadas?"

"No, punk, I mean Mexican frijoles a la charra."

"Sure. Whatever. I'll make you all the habichuelas you want."

We both laughed, and he put his arms around me until we fell asleep.

AVALANCHE I

Snow slab breaks between my knuckles
    Snowflakes flurry through blocked veins

Glaciers graze against crumbling finger slopes
    Ice pummels down a mountain bone of flesh

Frost cracks the nipple open, warps toes & bleeds lips
    I scratch the blue into purple until red returns

Dig under my nails for saltwater sand
    Find the ash of an avalanche buried beneath

Raise my palms & pull at the rays of the sun
    Hold in my hands the memory of warmth

HANDS CLEAN

THREE YEARS AFTER DIAGNOSIS, an ulcer appeared on the tip of my right middle finger. It was subtle, but it worried me just the same. Lupe and I had just recently gotten engaged, and I had moved in with him to save money for the wedding. One evening, while watching TV after dinner, I shoved my finger in Lupe's face and told him to look at it. He pulled his head back, held the finger between is thumb and forefinger, kissed my fingertip and assured me it was just a callus.

I sat down on the other end of the couch and continued to pick at the scabs, the skin and the nail. I wanted to find anything that would confirm my suspicions. I'd done the research and he hadn't.

After a while, when he still hadn't said anything to calm my obvious fears, I stared him down from across the couch. Feeling the burning glare, he looked up at me and sighed, knowing what I needed to hear.

"Well, if it is an ulcer, do you think you should see the doctor?"

"I don't know." I shrugged in an effort to get him to tell me what to do, so I wouldn't have to figure it out myself.

"Well, just leave it alone and we'll wait and see what happens."

"Okay, but what if . . . "

"For now, keep your hands clean."

"But, what if . . . "

"Jasminne, stop. Just stop. Keep it clean and warm and dry so it doesn't get infected. That's what the doctors always told you to do, right?"

There, he finally said it, the dreaded word "infected." It's what we both feared for reasons we couldn't even begin to understand yet. The Raynaud's phenomenon from my scleroderma caused my fingers to turn white and blue, and go numb in cold temperatures. That was the first symptom that had sent me to see a doctor in the first place and the one that currently seemed to be the most painful. The doctor had kindly informed me on numerous occasions that, "As long as I don't get any ulcers on my fingertips, Raynaud's wasn't dangerous." Well, there it was, an ulcer. If the ulcer were to get infected and did not get treated properly, it could lead to gangrene. Gangrene could lead to infection in the bone, and bone infections almost always led to amputation.

Although the threat of infection and amputation were very frightening, it was not what scared me the most. I feared not being able to write anymore. I feared depression. I feared not being able to dress myself or feed myself or hold his sweaty hands. I feared he would leave me for someone with all her digits intact and a body that wasn't slowly wasting away. I feared brokenness and tears. I feared impending idleness and his rejection.

At the time, I didn't know what Lupe was afraid of, because I hadn't found the courage to ask him yet. I needed to believe he was strong enough to handle all of this for the both of us, in case there came a time when I no longer could.

I held my finger, holding back tears that I didn't want to release so he wouldn't have to ask me what was wrong. I wanted to cry because my finger itched, because the TV was loud and I couldn't hear myself think, because I wanted it all in to be in my head. I wanted Lupe to be right because I didn't want to lose my fingers. I needed my hands to write, to teach, to hold his hand and to live.

He saw my eyes watering, got up and whispered in my ear, "You'll be fine."

I made myself believe him.

WHEN YOU MARRY A MEXICAN AMERICAN

Be prepared to eat
his hands, his smell, his Indio hair, his knuckles,
his politics, his scabs, his scars, his pain,
his bent back and taut shoulders, his ears, his history,
his tortilla gut filled with corridos and tequila.
Eat his skin every day so it doesn't leave your body,
swallow his breath into yours until you've made water into wine
& get drunk in each other's arms.
Choke on your words when you spite him.
Eat his touch, his taste, his eyes, his harmony & his discord.
Eat him till he craves you and feeds on both your wants.

Be prepared to cook
love into his voice with a bowl of menudo.
Sauté cebolla and chile in a pan until it wears you.
Grind garlic and joy into a stone molcajete
even when your wrists hurt from rubbing
his pain and his shirt necks clean.
Find pozole in his eyes and pour it
into your heart when the monotony of winter
mornings threatens to chill the burn between you.
Make love to tamales with your hands so when you touch
him he will always find a home there.

Be prepared to pray
with his mother, his tías, his primas,
his hermanas, his primas-hermanas.
Pray over dinner, in cornfields, on knees,
on horseback and in pickups. Reza
como si fuera la primera y última vez si él te lo pide.
Reza con aleluya y amén aunque él no crea en Dios
si él te lo pide. Pray in English or in Spanish or in Spanglish
even if you don't know the words.

Murmur the hum of the vowels in your throat
like a mantra if he asks you to. Pray with your pride
and his rosary in your hands. Pray until you become
the miracle he needs.

Be prepared to dance
into disagreements around the family table.
Stomp out regret and spin out your anger.
Dance your children into being.
Dance your ancestors out of the grave.
Dance until the music drowns you in sweat.
Let him dip and lead you.
Get lost in the drums & find your way back
to the beat of the single heart dwelling in your shared last name.
Grab hold of the back of his neck, kiss his lips
& bless yourself with his song.

Be prepared to listen
to heavy breathing when you watch him sleep.
Listen for his grieving.
Listen to his canas that inherited trauma and orgullo.
Listen to his Tejano tongue & sigh into his mariachi footsteps
every time he comes home from work.
Escucha lo que te dice con su sonrisa.
Escucha lo que oculta de su padre y lo que recuerda de su madre.
Hear his name in a brindis and know that his ¡SALUD!
will heal all your open wounds.

Be prepared to laugh
at the bills, the mortgage, the best laid plans, the tears,
the last bite of food, the first bite of dessert, the dishes,
the laundry, the dogs, the children or the lack thereof.
Ríanse a carcajadas de la enfermedad, la tristeza,
el dinero, el reguero, la libertad y el amor.
Chuckle even when your eyes water.

Giggle when he forgets the milk, your medicine,
your birthday, his keys, his lunch, your lunch, his faults,
your faults or even your maiden name.
Laugh every day before he walks out the door
so you can be sure joy is the only sound echoed between you.

SUPPORT GROUP

DOMINICANS DON'T DO THERAPY or seek counseling for their personal problems, at least not from anyone other than Jesus. If your immediate family can't fix it, then you're told to go pray about it. If you seek the advice or medical help of a professional for your emotional problems, you could be labeled "la loca," or worse yet, be accused of airing your family's dirty laundry con un desconocido. Which is the worst betrayal of all because of el que dirán.

But because Dominicans would also be the first to judge your feelings and rarely know how to just listen without interjecting something, I needed someone to talk to who would understand and empathize, not try to cure me with a remedio casero, a Holy Bible or a lecture about how, if I'd learned to cook "real" food and stop eating so much comida en la calle, I'd be better by now. Everyone had good intentions, but they never really listened.

I decided to seek help, but couldn't afford a therapist and really wanted a chance to meet other people who knew what it felt like to live with my kind of chronic illness and pain. I figured the next best thing to a personal therapist was a support group.

When I first told Lupe that I was going to go to a support group, he was thrilled. He knew it would help me. He knew there were parts of my illness he would never fully understand. He knew that connecting with other people who shared my struggle would help me cope. He told me that if I ever wanted him to come with me, he would, but that he understood if I needed this time for myself to be able to say or talk about what I wanted. It was exactly what I needed to hear.

After a few sessions, I decided to tell Mami about my support group meetings. I knew she would find out somehow in the way mom's find out everything—through a sibling, a look from your tía at dinner or a Facebook post you forgot to delete. But when I told her, I didn't exactly say it was a support group. I didn't want her to think our conversations or daily check-ins weren't enough for my mental and emotional health. I didn't want to listen to another sermon about how I just needed to have a little more faith en Dios, and everything would be fine. Instead, I told her a half truth.

We were on the phone on one of our daily calls, when she asked me how I was feeling. "¿Cómo sigues? ¿Te sientes bien?"

"Más o menos. I dunno. Just feeling kind of sad, I guess. I don't know if la medicina is helping. I'm just so tired all the time."

I could hear the water running in the background. She was washing dishes with the phone pressed between her ear and shoulder as she scrubbed off grease caked on a silver pan.

"¿Pero por qué? ¿Por qué te sientes así?"

I wasn't sure if she'd heard the last part of my statement or if she really just expected me to be okay. I never was really good at sharing my feelings with Mami, not in Spanish anyway, and what I wanted to say in English I didn't think she would understand.

I sighed and changed the subject. "I'm going to go to a . . . a meeting next Saturday."

She turned off the faucet and I heard a pot clang. I pulled the phone away from my ear. "Ma!"

"Ay, perdón. ¿Qué dices? ¿Vas a ir a una meeting? ¿De qué?"

"Es una reunión. For patients with scleroderma. Para conocer a otros pacientes. Just to learn more about the disease and to talk, you know. They have snacks, a presentation and you meet people."

"¿Oh, sí? ¿En Houston?"

"Sí."

"Yo quiero ir. Yo y tu papá vamos a ir. Y si él no quiere ir, yo me voy sola."

Shit, I thought. Of course, she wanted to come. Dominicans love to socialize en familia, and I had made a support group meeting sound like a damn social hour.

"Ma, that's not necessary. You don't need to drive three hours for some two-hour meeting. It's no big deal."

Her pitch raised and she exhaled. "¿Qué, no quieres que vaya? Está bien. No voy."

She had hit me with Mami guilt. I could feel it pummeling through the airwaves, traveling almost 300 miles out of her kitchen sink and into the pit of my stomach.

"No. Está bien. Sí, ya'll should come," I said resigned.

"Qué bueno. Nos vemos el viernes por la noche."

And just like that, Mami was coming to my support group meeting.

🌿 🌿 🌿

I asked Lupe to come with us that Saturday because, when he was around my parents, things just felt easier and less dramatic. Lupe had a way of making everyone laugh and distracting us with elaborate stories about his classroom and his students. He also helped diffuse my frustrations and calm Mami's nerves when she wanted to know how I was "really" doing.

That Saturday morning, after a hearty breakfast of mangú y huevos revueltos, we piled into the car and headed to Northwest Hospital where the Scleroderma Foundation held monthly patient information sessions and support group meetings. The information session was to be led by a doctor from Dallas on the varying degrees of skin involvement in the disease. I knew this would be of special interest to Papi because he had acquired the bad habit of grabbing me by the forearms and assessing my skin every time he saw me, without even so much as a hello or a hug first. I knew it was his way of saying he cared about me and was worried, but I wished he would just ask me how I was doing rather than try to diagnose me based on the texture of my skin.

Before the information session began, patients and their families socialized for a bit, snacked on food and surveyed the pamphlet table. I knew a few of the patients there from previous meetings and said hello. It was good to see familiar faces. I introduced Mami, Papi and Lupe, and several of the patients were struck by how "blessed" I was to have so many people at my side. It hadn't dawned on me that arriving with a crew would garner admiration. What I saw as an embarrassing inconvenience actually made me enviable.

In support group meetings, I could usually find the same types of people. We all usually fit into one category or another, and, at each meeting, I always seemed to find myself moving into a new category. That day wasn't much different. The types of people that attended the support group included:

1) The Newbie: A patient who was probably newly or recently diagnosed, or had had the disease for many years but had just decided to get informed and seek help. This type of person would either stay quiet and listen or would divulge their entire chronic illness story in the first five minutes. Often still in denial, they believed that they couldn't possibly have this disease and/or that all doctors were useless, and they needed to get a third, fourth and fifth opinion despite the fact that their symptoms were similar to or exactly like everyone else's in the room. At one point I was that person, but that phase didn't last long. I knew what it was like to be the newbie, so I always made an effort to talk to and meet any new person in the group.

2) The Know It All: An individual who had studied every pamphlet and WebMD article, had been to numerous specialists and insisted that their current one was the best and you should get an appointment with them ASAP. This person liked to tell others what they could and could/should not do or take but immediately qualified their aggressive statements with phrases like, "Well that was my experience" or "Everyone is different, I know" or "You do what you want and what is best for you, but . . . " These types of folks were helpful when they weren't being arrogant or pushy.

3) The Holy Roller: Someone who quoted the Bible and believed that, by the power of the Holy Spirit, we would all be saved and cured. These people always invited me to church with them and asked me about my relationship with God. While I was spiritual and prayed often, I didn't expect God to cure me or bless me with the miracle of remission.

4) The Optimist: The one who was always chipper and decided that laughter and joy were the best medicine. Their illness had

opened their eyes to what was really important in life, and now everything was sunshine and sprinkles. These people had usually taken everything in life well, and this wasn't an exception. Lupe was like that, but I wasn't. I longed to feel joy and hope, no matter what, but it was a daily struggle, and sometimes I wasn't given the choice. On days when I woke up feeling too tired or too pained to even brush my teeth, my whole mood waned and wouldn't lift as long as the fatigue kept me in bed.

5) The Crier: This person was also usually the newbie and sat at the opposite end of the scale to the optimist. The crier rarely spoke at the meeting, and when they did, all they could do was cry. They insisted on wanting to know why. Why them? Why this disease? I was this person too, for a while, until the "what now" began to matter more than the "why."

6) The Hopeless: This was someone who let everyone know how miserable they were about their condition. They needed real one-on-one help, not a support group. Their grief sank deep, and you could see it in their gray expressions and clouded eyes. They didn't cry like the crier did. They were out of tears, resigned to pain and perhaps had even stopped taking their medications because they no longer saw the point. I tried to be especially gentle with these types. I said hello softly, made eye contact, asked to bring them a drink or a snack. If they spoke, I made sure to listen fully without interrupting. I knew they were fragile. Because I assumed I would be there too one day, I did my best to help them hold their grief.

7) The Solicitor: Also almost always a woman, loaded with catalogues and samples of whatever she was selling. She used the meetings to earn a living. She may have been sick or had a family member that she was there "to support." I avoided this person at all costs because I always had a hard time saying no to things and people who smiled at me. I knew I'd end up buying something I didn't need.

8) The Walk-A-Thoner and/or Motivational Speaker: Their wardrobe consisted of fundraising T-shirts, hats, backpacks, lanyards and other find-a-cure, non-profit paraphernalia. They

believed that a cure was possible. Every year, for every event, they would walk/run/bowl/bike to find it. They would also likely share Oprah or Deepak Chopra platitudes like, "Your life is yours, own it and take control" or, "In the midst of movement and chaos, keep stillness inside of you." Then they would share some part of their illness "journey" and how anything could be possible with the right mindset and motivation. After all, just look at how well they're doing. Half the time I wanted to punch these people in the face because their "inspiration" seemed so fabricated. I imagined they went home and cried themselves to sleep every night. I didn't understand whom this display of energy and strength was for. Wasn't this also just another manifestation of denial?

9) The Herbalist: A person who would tell you that all their aches, pains, problems, stress and anxiety had been cured with lavender oil and organic apple cider vinegar. They insisted that "toxic" drugs and western medicine were not the answer. Everyone should replace their general practitioner or specialist with an acupuncturist and yoga. While I did give all of these alternative therapies a try, and some did work for certain symptoms, I knew western medicine was the only thing that would be able to suppress my immune system enough to allow me to function. I desperately wished green tea and meditation would cure me because I, too, hated taking toxic medications that had deadly side effects. But I also feared death and disability, and no alternative treatment had proven as effective as my rheumatologist's concoctions of medications.

10) The Silent: Said nothing and sat quietly. Didn't want to be noticed and left early.

11) The Support Group Junkie: A person who attended every support group meeting they had a diagnosis for and wanted to feel connected and understood by others. Likely kept a blog or followed at least a dozen of them. Spent their evenings responding to online support group forum questions and giving friendly advice to strangers all over the world. I was becoming one of these people. But it was the only thing I felt like I could do that made a

difference. I wanted my illness to mean something. I wanted to make a difference. So I started a blog. I wrote poems and shared them at a fundraiser. I answered people's questions online as if I were an expert. It made the experience of living with the illness less empty.

12) The Mooch: A person who was only there for the food. They would fill their tiny appetizer plate with cheese, crackers, fruit and cookies and would go back for seconds and thirds during the meeting. At this Saturday's meeting, Papi became the mooch. I think it was because when it came time for the support group meeting, he was uneasy about being in a room full of people willing to share their feelings and food was how we coped in my family.

13) The Loved One: This could be a mom, husband, sister or friend of a patient. They came alone because their sick loved one refused to come or couldn't physically make it there. The loved one came because they needed to understand what it was like to live with the disease in order to try and empathize with their sick family member. They wanted to know what worked for others in order to try and convince their loved one that it could work for them too. Fatigue weighed on their shoulders and dragged in their feet. They were desperate to find a cure or a treatment plan that could make their beloved who they were before. They needed to talk to someone because their loved ones wouldn't talk to them.

And then there was me. I always found myself in a new category or floating between two or three of them at a time. Illness and disease were still new in my body and in my identity. Because I was also usually one of only two women of color in the room, this added to the burden of feeling like an outsider in a place where I was supposed to feel like everyone else.

By arriving to the meeting with Mami, Papi and Lupe, I realized I had created my own category: The Entourage. What I had expected was two hours of embarrassing questions from Papi, a stress-inducing and tear-filled outburst from Mami and a few futile attempts from Lupe to keep the peace. But actually, the meeting was the first step on the road to healing. As Mami, Papi, Lupe and, eventually, my sis-

ter Jennifer came to these informational sessions and monthly support group meetings, we became closer as a family. The sessions
often led to tears and hugs, laughter and enlightenment. Papi would
feel satisfied that he had learned a new word or could identify a new
symptom. Mami enjoyed watching me make friends and that everyone knew my name. Lupe always asked the hard questions and
would make everyone in the room laugh when he told stories about
the time when he told me not to eat pizza and I didn't listen and we
both stayed up all night dealing with my heartburn and gas, or how
he had nicknamed me "bullet wound" because I treated every ache
and pain as if I had been shot. I became the one with the entourage,
and if they happened not to come to a meeting, someone always
asked why.

With Mami, Papi and Lupe at my side that day, each playing their
respective parts as caregivers, answer-seekers and advocates for my
health, I realized that I already had an army of support lined up
behind me before I even entered the room. I had been trying to spare
them from fully experiencing my grief because I was trying to protect
them from my hurt. I wanted to shield them from feeling disappointed in themselves. I didn't want them to carry any blame. But what I
needed to do was let them work through their hurt and their loss,
however they needed to, not the way I wanted them to. And that
meant that Papi would need to ask embarrassing questions and check
my skin, Mami would need to pray and cook me a hot meal and Lupe
would need to tell funny stories and hug me as tight as I could let him.

We sat down before the session began. My entourage and I took
up a whole row. I realized that my support group had always been
there. Even when I tried to be independent and push them away, they
weren't going anywhere. I was surrounded by loved ones in my life
that didn't need to sit in a circle to be a part of one. And unlike so
many of the types of people I encountered in the scleroderma and
chronic pain support groups who had spouses and parents and siblings
who just didn't understand their disease, I was lucky enough to have
people in my life who were eager to be involved and desperate to be
a part of every aching, bleeding, uncertain and wonderful moment.

PART II: RED JASMIN(N)E

plant me in fertile ground
near a garden womb wall I climb
until all you see is red

FIRST TRIMESTER

First it was one blue river line & then it was two—until
   I found blood between my legs without a wound.

First it was pomegranate purple & then it charred black—until
   I knelt in midnight prayer & the earth beneath me cracked.

First my womb swarmed grey a cackle of bleeding cicadas—until
   I dug one out & buried it to make room for you.

First I blessed myself with breast milk from an ocean shore & then
   I hung a wreath of obsidian diapers on the nursery door.

First I built an altar for the name I would not give you & then
   I lit a candle for when I carried it in my womb.

ONE IN FOUR

Expel: *force out or reject from the body, eject, discharge.*
One in four pregnancies end in a miscarriage. A miscarriage is
the expulsion of a fetus from the womb before it can survive on its
own. If one in four pregnancies ended in a miscarriage, why didn't I
know it could happen to me?

❦ ❦ ❦

The dread of going into work sat like a heavy meal in my stomach all morning before I got up. This was unusual for me, because I normally loved going into the classroom to see my students. But that morning I felt off kilter. My muscles ached a bit from exhausting myself over the weekend, and I was worried about a flare up. My new full-time job as a drama and speech teacher was stressful, keeping up with the house was impossible, and we had found out I was pregnant just a few weeks earlier and the uncertainty of what nine months of pregnancy would do to my body was overwhelming. My scleroderma didn't respond well to stress, and a flare up would mean my chronic fatigue, muscle aches and joint pain could come back and knock me out at any time. All I needed and wanted was some mental and physical rest.

When the alarm went off, I groaned and pulled the covers tight over my body and leaned in to kiss Lupe. He moaned and stroked my shoulder.

I whispered in his ear, "I gotta get up."

"Okay, " he said, "I need five more minutes."

"Okay, but can you take the dog out today? I don't want to be late."

"Yeah, that's fine." He turned over to keep sleeping.

I sat up and my feet dangled over the side of our king-sized bed. I breathed in and out and repeated my daily affirmation, "All is well in my world. I move forward in life with comfort and ease." I used this as a reminder to myself that everything was going to be okay, even if it wasn't. I placed my bare feet on the cold tile floor and walked to the bathroom.

I started to pee. What normally felt like an exhilarating release of all the restlessness from the night before actually felt heavier and unpleasant as it left my body. What came out of me stung and burned. I wiped myself clean and saw that the toilet paper was covered in blood. Like the time I got my first period, this was not what I expected. This was not the kind of transition or rite of passage I had ever wanted. My stomach clenched. What I had known for weeks in my heart suddenly materialized in the flesh. My baby was gone. Peeing on a stick had confirmed that I was carrying life. And now, in this urine sample, that same life was coming to an end.

I stared down at the soiled toilet paper. What once was white and smooth, was now covered in my self-aborted fetus' blood. A crimson red syrup seeped between the crevices and black clotted remnants of a heart that would never beat stuck to the crumpled sheets of Quilted Northern I held in my hand.

As my heart began to harden, the paper felt soft in my hands. I didn't want to throw it away for fear of losing the only physical evidence I would ever have of having been a mother. But I did. And it floated there for a moment, like a deflated raft lost at sea. The expelled fetus stared back at me, taunting, "You just tossed me away, Mother, how could you just toss me away?" I flushed it down and screamed for Lupe.

🌸

Abnormal*: unusual, uncommon, freak, freakish, rare, isolated in a way that is undesirable or worrying.*

One in four pregnancies end in miscarriage. Usually the cause of miscarriage is unknown. Miscarriage is nature's way of ending a pregnancy that is abnormal or would not make it to term. Our baby would not make it to term. What was wrong with our baby?

❧   ❧   ❧

I held onto the sink as the bathroom walls began to spin. Lupe rushed in.

"What's the matter? What happened?" He stood next to me and put his hand on my shoulder.

"I need to go to the ER. Right now!"

"Babe, what happened?! What's going on?"

"I don't know! I'm bleeding. Like a lot. And I know it can't be normal."

"Okay. Okay. I'll take you. Let me get dressed and we'll go. I'll bring you some clothes to change into. Just go sit in the living room."

I went instead to the bedroom to grab my phone from the night-stand. I knew I would have to call in to work, but I didn't even know what I would say. My hands shook, my mind a flurry of thoughts and emotions I couldn't contain. I swatted blindly for words to make sense of what I felt, but they evaded me like flies buzzing around a rotted carcass. I called the front office.

"Good morning, thank you for calling Jesuit Preparatory, this is Kimberly, how may I help you."

"Hi, Kim, it's Mrs. Méndez. Um, I can't come in today. Canyou-pleasegetmeasub?" The words shot out of me in one breath, popping like balloons with every syllable uttered. I had spoken too loudly, too frantically, too desperately for 6 am.

"Oh," she paused, "okay, Mrs. Méndez. Is everything all right?"

She had asked the one question I needed her not to ask. Tears gushed from my eyes like water from a busted fire hydrant on a hot summer day.

"Um, I can't really talk about it right now." My voice shook, my hands trembled and I reached for the bed, only to have my legs give in to the sinkhole of emotions that suddenly overcame me. My knees hit the floor, and I began to sob.

"Don't worry about it. I hope everything is okay. I'll get a sub for you. Have a good day."

"Thank you."

I hung up. I walked to the living room and sat down. I held my belly. I felt one thousand tiny men kicking away at my stomach. I doubled over and rocked myself back and forth.

"No. Please, God. No."

As a last ditch effort, I said a silent prayer in the form of a lullaby to stifle the truth I could no longer ignore. My baby was gone.

"Here," Lupe said, handing me some clothes. "Get dressed."

I did, and he helped me to the door and into the car.

❦

Spontaneous: unplanned, unrehearsed, occurring as a result of a sudden inner impulse or without obvious external cause.

One in four pregnancies end in a miscarriage. A miscarriage is rarely ever anyone's fault. There is usually nothing a woman or doctor could have done to prevent a miscarriage or save the fetus. The medical term for a miscarriage is spontaneous abortion. I had always been a planner. This pregnancy was planned. The miscarriage was not.

❦ ❦ ❦

As Lupe drove me to the ER, I thought about how something that was barely beginning was already coming to an end. I thought about our oceanic, king-sized bed, where it all began and where it had ended. It was a bed Lupe hated because his feet did not reach the floor when he sat on it. It was a bed I chose before we got married because my body ached every morning when I got up from his bachelor pad blue futon and I couldn't take it anymore. It was the bed where we often consummated our marriage and eventually conceived the baby I was now losing. It was also the place where only two weeks before all the blood and sadness consumed me, I had felt a sharp pain in my abdomen. It was a slow rip that pulled through my stomach from left to right, like the slow tear of a plantain peel. I then felt several shooting cramps in my lower belly that hugged my insides and wrapped around my waist. I had a feeling then that something was happening and so I held my belly and said, "No." I held my baby even tighter and said, "I love you." And after a few deep breaths, I held myself and said, "Okay." I had felt seasick, so I curled up in the fetal position, like a crab holed up in her shell beneath the waves of sheets that covered the ocean expanse of our bed, and I affirmed my beliefs: "All is well in my world. All is well in my world."

I knew then that the pregnancy was over. But I was not ready to accept it yet. It had only been a few days before that I felt the cramping we had gone to the OB/GYN for the six-week ultrasound. We were excited. It was my first time being pregnant in the first month of us "trying," and I believed all was well. I believed it had to be because I had already been through so much in the last five years with my chronic illnesses. This just had to be the one thing in my life that would go well, the thing that would finally bring me some peace and joy.

The day of the ultrasound, we went into the exam room. I disrobed and put on a paper gown. Lupe sat down next to me and held my hand until the nurse came back into the room. At six weeks, they had to do a transvaginal ultrasound, because the embryo was too small to be seen from the abdomen.

I spread my legs as wide as my tight scleroderma-scarred hips would let me and took a deep breath. She went in and stared up at the image on the screen. Lupe and I looked up too. We didn't know what we were supposed to see but we should have heard a heartbeat.

The nurse asked, "When was your last menstrual period?"

"November 6th. It started November 6th."

"Are you sure?"

"Yes, because it was my birthday."

"Hmm. Well I don't hear a heartbeat yet. Are you sure you are six weeks along? The size of the sac looks more like four."

"I'm sure. My last cycle started on November 6th." But even I was beginning to doubt it and was suddenly nervous.

"Well, it could just be that you conceived later than you thought. Or it might be a blighted ovum. But we won't know for sure until we run some tests and wait it out to see if your hCG levels increase. All right?"

She removed the ultrasound device from inside me, cleaned it off, removed her blue latex gloves and said she'd be right back.

"I don't understand what's happening." I sat up, exposed in my paper gown, still holding Lupe's hand.

"Well, like she said, we just wait and see. I'm sure everything is fine. Maybe we just miscalculated everything."

"But I'm sure I had my period on the sixth. It started on my birthday. I remember that." I was growing anxious.

"That's fine, I believe you. Don't get upset. We just have to wait and see."

They did the bloodwork. I was sent home. I waited for the results. The next day, a nurse called me: "Your hCG levels are rising. Everything should be fine."

I assumed everything would be fine.

※

Blighted: infected, to spoil, harm, mildew or destroy.

One in four pregnancies end in a miscarriage. A blighted ovum causes about one out of every two miscarriages in the first trimester. A blighted ovum is when a gestational sac forms and grows but an embryo does not develop. Where had my baby gone? Was my baby ever really there? Why was there nothing left of my baby to bury beneath the soil?

※ ※ ※

At the ER, the nurse practitioner did an ultrasound, a pelvic exam, drew some blood from my temperamental veins and confirmed a miscarriage likely due to a blighted ovum. I sat up in the gurney and remained silent. Lupe tried to hug me, but I couldn't lift my arms. I heard the deafening swish and crackle of the paper sheet beneath me, and it made me cringe. I could not look him in the eye. What had I done? Why was his baby gone? We had created life, but I was only to give birth to death. I sobbed into his shoulder.

The nurse came back in and told me to see my OB the next day to follow up and ensure I had "expelled all fetal tissue."

After a couple of hours of waiting on test results, we were sent home to rest. For the next 48 hours at home and after I was admitted to the hospital for observation, I expelled blood. I expelled sweat that dripped out of every pore when the cramps overcame every fiber of my being and doubled me over in pain. Into a dingy pillow, I expelled tears that would eventually be stifled for fear I had grieved too long, only to flood my heart and my lungs with fluid that would threaten to drown me from the inside out. Finally, into a plastic bucket that hovered over a hospital toilet, I expelled, and the nurses collected the last bit of the someone else I would never get to meet.

❦

_____ : *There is no word in English or Spanish for a parent who has lost a child. There is no word in English or Spanish for a woman who once was pregnant and suddenly is not. One in four pregnancies end in a miscarriage. We named our child Baby M so we had a name for our grief, a word for our loss.*

❦ ❦ ❦

On January 4, 2012, the night before my miscarriage, my god-daughter was born. Lupe and I decided to go meet her and congratulate the new parents. We had been close friends with them for many years and were thrilled to welcome their daughter, Juliet, into the world. Before heading up to the room, we stopped at the gift shop in the hospital. We chose rose-colored balloons, an over-priced bouquet of pink and yellow carnations and a card with a smiling brown bear on the cover flap with "Congratulations" printed in Monotype Corsiva on the inside.

Thirty-six dollars and 89 cents later, we were on the elevator up to the seventh floor, the maternity wing of The Women's Hospital of Texas. It was then that I felt something inside me going really wrong. I stared into the rose-colored balloons I held up in front of my face and took a deep breath.

"Are you okay?" Lupe asked, sensing that something was wrong.

"I don't know." I really didn't know.

"What's wrong?"

"Earlier today, before we left the house, when I wiped, there was some blood," I paused. "And I think I'm bleeding a little now."

"Oh. Well, do you just want to go home and rest?"

"No, no. We're already here. Besides, I want to meet the baby."

"Okay. Well, we don't have to stay long. Visiting hours end in 30 minutes, anyway. And if you want, we can go see the doctor tomorrow." He squeezed my shoulder.

"Okay."

I took a deep breath. The sweet smell of the carnations, which failed to mask the smell of sterile hand sanitizer that permeated every corner of the hospital, sickened me and made my eyes water. I couldn't get out of that elevator fast enough.

Baby Juliet's room overflowed with family, friends and unadulterated love. Because that's what babies did. They made you feel love. For yourself, for each other and for humanity. After all, weren't babies God's way of telling us that the world should go on? So I couldn't help but wonder: what did it mean when a baby died?

The baby's father, Xavier, interrupted my existential thoughts. "Hey! The Méndez's are here!"

He greeted us and took the gifts from our hands. "Come in, she's awake."

"Hi, everyone." I forced a half smile and squeezed my way into the crowded room.

Xavier's girlfriend, Michelle, was lying in the bed, holding baby Juliet. She smiled at me and asked how I was doing.

"I'm okay. How are you?" I clutched my purse tightly, trying to sound as upbeat as possible.

"We're fine. Just really tired," said Michelle.

"I bet."

I walked up closer to the bed and peered over at the pink bundle she held in her arms. "Hi, Juliet. Welcome to the world." I squeezed one of her tiny hands to keep myself from crying.

"You want to hold her?"

"Um, sure. I guess." I had never held a newborn before, at least not one that was only a few hours old, and it made me nervous. I didn't know what to do, and I think it showed.

"Don't be nervous. Just be sure you hold her head."

Michelle handed me the baby gently, and I cradled her in my arms. I felt her warmth against my breast, and my heart pounded rhythmically against her soft pink temple. I inhaled her and stroked the three strands of hair that covered her forehead. Then Juliet wiggled in my arms and made me laugh. Everyone around me was chatting, but all I heard then was Juliet's soft breath against my chest.

BABY M
11/2011-01/2012

BABY M died in the womb at five weeks gestation. He/she was conceived by loving parents in November of 2011. The cause of Baby M's death is unknown.

Every year on January 4th, a moment of silence is observed at the home of Lupe and Jasminne Méndez.

NOT YET

I SAT IN A GREY CHAIR wearing a grey dress, surrounded by purple walls and a room full of women. I shook. I took my pills that morning on an empty stomach. I was paying the price dearly for that mistake. My eyes blinked as if in slow motion. I bit my lip. Everyone and everything in the room seemed completely surreal. They called my name, and I signed in and paid the $25 copay. I held my purse close; it was the only thing I was certain of. I texted Lupe and told him I was expecting the worst. Because expecting and hoping for the best would only lead to more disappointment. He told me to call him when it was all over.

"All over, all over," I repeated in my head. As if I weren't already.

I contemplated picking up a *WebMd* or *Mommy and Me* magazine but decided against it. I refused to give into torture. I looked around the room some more; there were four women bursting with life. I clutched my purse to my empty stomach. I managed to avert everyone's eyes, except those of a cute four-year-old girl. Her smile and eyes found me.

She looked like me, only prettier. Light brown frizzy hair, beautiful hazelnut skin and a bit of sass in her hips. She walked towards me. I looked at her mother. The mother didn't say anything to me or the child, so I said hello to the little girl. She brought over a magazine and began to point at the pictures. I helped her name the objects she didn't know.

"That's a penny. That's a key, a lock, a screwdriver, a . . . "

"A MONKEY!" she interrupted enthusiastically.

"Yes, that's right."

I forced a smile and she turned the pages. She pointed to things she didn't know the names of, and I gave them a name. She pointed at animals and named them all. I smiled. *I would be a good mom*, I thought, *I knew I would.*

"How old are you?" I asked.

She quickly looked over at her mom. The mother was busy on her phone. The little girl shrugged her shoulders.

"Are you five?"

"No."

"Are you four?"

She nodded yes and looked back at her mom. Her mother still didn't notice.

"Why are you here?" the little girl asked me.

"I'm here to see the doctor," I said.

"Oh. Why?"

"Just to make sure I'm healthy."

"Oh. Is there a baby in your tummy, too?"

I paused. My lip trembled. The mother finally looked up from her phone and smiled at me.

"No. Not yet," I said.

A look of confusion swept across her face. "Oh."

And we smiled to break the tension.

I had told her, "Not yet," when the truth was, "Not anymore."

INSANITY

*"... is doing the same thing over and over
and expecting different results."*

—Albert Einstein

I held the pissed-stained stick in my hands and sank to the bath-room floor. The first response on the home pregnancy test revealed only one line, again.

WHAT TO EXPECT WHEN YOU'RE NOT EXPECTING
Why did I keep failing at this?

MONTH AFTER MONTH, I changed my strategy. Sex right before ovulation. Sex on the day of ovulation. Sex the day after ovulation and three more days after that. Lubricant. No lubricant. Knees up in the air for 30 minutes, pillow under my ass. Didn't pee right after sex. Didn't douche. Did acupuncture. Didn't stress. Practiced yoga. Drank the "Fertilitea." Swallowed my pride and vitamins. Meditated and just stopped trying.

What was I doing wrong?

Tears. Home pregnancy tests. Ovulation kits. Tears. Stress. Dryness. Sex. Strawberries, whip cream and sex. Lit candles. Sex. Lights on. Lights off. Sex. More tears. Frustration. Anger. Lubrication. No lubrication. Pre-seed lubrication. Stress. Sex. Tears. Blood. Tampons. Pads. More home pregnancy sticks. Palm readings. Sex. Prayers. Tears. Stress. Sex. Sweat. Tears.

Why couldn't anyone help me?

Blogs and discussion boards. Two therapists. Silence. Friends who understood. Friends who didn't. Mom. Tía. Cousins. Girl's night out. Group therapy. Maternal fetal medicine specialist. Support group. Silence. Lupe held me. Silence. Fertility counselor. Music. Chocolate. Chat rooms. Lupe kissed me. Friends. Mothers. Spinsters. Silence. Adoption agent. Surrogacy websites. Text messages. Lupe sighed. Phone calls. Me. Silence.

DAR A LUZ

Like La Llorona I weep
"Ay, ay, ay . . ."
                              I am

infertile.   A womb
of skin & blood & bone stitched
to wind & words & dust. "I'm pregnant,"

la comadre announces
to me and the kitchen walls
on the 4th of July.   I feel light

leave my body. I wipe my sticky
watermelon hands on an apron and reach out
to hug the ice chest.   I lift

its dead weight across the room
near the only plant I've ever kept
alive.   I check

its soil for moisture. My fingers curl
into being beneath the dirt.
"Congratulations,"   I say

my necrotic tongue sticks
to my teeth. La comadre listens for a pulse
in my breathing.   I muffle

heartache on the inhale.
Coke cans cackle. Melted ice caps
clap.   I'm startled

by a firework next door. "I just wanted you
to be the first to know," snaking around
like amniotic fluid.   I hide

the evidence of envy in my tear ducts.
I offer us a child-proof
smile. La comadre agrees.   I linger

in the space between   "I'm glad
you're okay . . . " & "Are you all right?"
Sunlight in a stained-glass window.

HOW TO BE INFERTILE

WILLINGLY PLAN YOUR SISTER'S or your best friend's baby shower, even if you have been trying to get pregnant since before either of them were married. Endure at least one miscarriage (if not more) and several years of negative pregnancy tests. While they buy maternity clothes and complain about swollen feet, continue to pee on ovulation predictor kits, track your cycle, have lots of sex, put pillows under your butt, take your basal temperature, swallow prenatal vitamins or Clomid or hormone pills, get acupuncture, practice yoga, drink Fertiliteas, avoid caffeine and alcohol, pray, meditate and try your damnedest to "relax and just stop trying."

Be happy for them. And most of the time, you really are. Because after all, how can you not celebrate the miracle that is conception and childbirth? You especially know how miraculous such a thing is, because at this point in your own journey towards motherhood, conceiving a child really would take a *miracle*. So, smile. Every time they post a baby bump picture on social media . . . smile. When they send you Pinterest photos of what the theme to their nursery will be . . . smile. When they send you the guest list to the baby shower you will spend your time and money on . . . smile. Because after all, the miracle of life is a blessing, and since you're not the one who's expecting, you must have all the time and money in the world . . . so . . . smile.

Next, make handmade crafty centerpieces, lick and stamp envelopes, order food and delegate tasks to soon-to-be grandmothers and other "besties" and sorority sisters. Find a venue or offer up your own home so that the mom-to-be simply has to show up, be pregnant and get showered with gifts. Plan three or four games to play, such as measure mommy's belly, guess mommy's weight, baby shower bingo, smell the dirty diaper and chug the juice from the bottle. Even though no one really likes these games, play them, because it's what you do at a baby shower. Decide to treat this whole charade like a game you know you have already lost.

❧

Sometimes in my dreams at night, I picture myself with a bun in the oven. I touch my belly and feel a kick. I hear old nursery rhymes clear as day:

Pat-a-cake, pat-a-cake, baker's man.
Bake me a cake as fast as you can

❧   ❧   ❧

If your sister or best friend lives close by and their spouses are unavailable, help them create the gift registry. She'll insist: It'll be fun! And you hope that it will be, for her sake and yours.

Pick her up and go to the store. Walk up and down isle after isle of baby clothes, shoes, trinkets, toys, devices, gadgets, car seats, strollers, cribs, diapers, linens, bottles, noisemakers, breast pumps and things you didn't even realize newborns and their mothers need. For a moment feel relieved that this is not your life, that you are not the one who is pregnant . . . for just one moment. Cringe when she squeals because she's found the perfect outfit to take baby home in after he/she is born. See it and squeal too. Smile and let your eyes light up and feel your heart split open like a lactating breast as you hold back tears. It is a baby blue/baby pink onesie with a warm hat and baby gloves. It is soft like fleece and smooth cotton. It is warm and smells like soft lavender and baby powder. Tell her it's perfect. Tell her you want to buy it for her. Find solace when she says thank you, thank you, thank you.

On the ride home from the store, let her fill the silence with the question neither of you wants to really talk about. Give her permission to be considerate. Empathize with the fact that she wants to be there for you like you have been there for her. Hold steady when she asks you, "How's it going?" She doesn't need to explain herself further; you both know what she's talking about. Act confident and composed and neutral. Tell her, "It's going fine." Tell her they still don't know what's wrong and you'll probably start fertility treatments soon, but you just can't afford it right now. Tell her that it's okay, because you and your spouse are focusing on other things. You're enjoying your marriage and your freedom, and besides, there's a lot going on right now. You just bought a house, or one of you just started a new job, or one of you needs to finish school, or honestly you just don't know if kids are even for you. Sigh when she tells you to stop talking nonsense. Avoid eye contact when she assures you that it will happen, that you will make a great mother. Accept that this is not the first or last time you will have this conversation.

Try to gather your scurried thoughts when she asks you again if you would consider adoption. Feel your heart sink further. You don't want to adopt. Not now, not ever. You want to carry a child in your womb. You want your fucking body to do the one the thing it is supposed to do. But do not say that right now. After all, she has taken a moment to consider your feelings. Do not get angry or sad during her time of joy. Do not upset her or the baby. Instead, grip the steering wheel and tell her maybe one day, but that adoption is expensive too. Find the courage to smile when she nods and tells you she's grateful to have you as a friend. Place your hand on her belly and promise to be the best auntie/godmother in the world.

I'd like to believe that my miscarried baby is out there in the universe somewhere. That if we as humans are made of the same stuff as the stars, then I'll see him when I look up. That if I wait long enough, we'll meet again.

Twinkle, twinkle, little star,
How I wonder what you are.

❧ ❧ ❧

The night before the shower, make sure everything is ready to go: the pink, blue, yellow or green plates and cups and napkins; the gift baskets, the crafty centerpieces, the cheese and cracker plates, the fruit and veggie plate, the diaper cake; the shower souvenirs, the balloons, the linens, the venue or your spotless home; your perfect outfit, shaved legs and flawless hair and, last but not least, your game face. Practice smiling in the mirror with your eyes, because you know your eyes will give it all away. Make your eyes glow and look joyful; no one should be able to see the sadness behind them. Do not risk making tomorrow about you. Only a few people even know you are also trying to have a baby, and you hope no one will bring it up. This can only happen if you actually look happy, if you can convince everyone including yourself that this day is only about the mom-to-be and her baby. Remind yourself all night long that tomorrow is not about you.

Don't sleep. Worry about every last detail. Let your spouse hold you for a while until you fall asleep. Feel the warmth and pray for it to be enough. Tell God or the universe or the darkness in the room that you don't want to want this anymore. Try to read but end up on your phone posting to infertility discussion boards or scrolling through your various social media accounts until your eyes glaze over, the sun comes up and the dogs need to be walked and fed. Get up early and fix things, load the car, get ready. Don't have the stomach to eat anything. Spend the day running on a few cups of tea or coffee because at this point you figure caffeine isn't what's keeping you from getting pregnant. Get dressed in the outfit you spent days perfecting, put on make-up, fix your hair and try smiling with your eyes one more time. See it, for a flash, a tinge of happiness echoing out of the corners of your eyes. Let it go.

Turn to look at your spouse when he checks on you. Let him hug you. Ache for what you cannot give him. Ache for the child you once carried and lost. Ache for the betrayal that is your body. Then try to hold yourself together in his arms. His warmth comforts you and his words of encouragement will help you make it through the day. He knows this is hard on you, but he knows you will be okay. Believe him.

Go to the party. Arrive early to set up and make sure everything is perfect. When the guests arrive, help them place their gifts on the gift table, show them to their seats, talk and laugh with them, soak in the admiration of their ooohs and aaahs at the decorations, the cupcake tower, the cookies, the theme and all the work and effort you have put into it. Hug the soon-to-be grandmother, who says everything is wonderful and beautiful and so perfect. Tell them it was fun. Tell them you love doing things like this. Tell them it was nothing.

When your sister or best friend arrives, listen to everyone cackle and squeal and clap with glee. Watch them hug her and touch her belly. Listen to them tell her she looks beautiful and is ready to pop. Swallow hard when everyone laughs. Show her to her seat and offer her a plate of food. As she eats, she will also oooh and aaah at everything you have done and thank you. She will tell you she feels special and lucky to have you in her life. Tell her you would do anything for her.

As the party goes on, play the games, refill the drinks, tell the stories of your best friend before marriage and motherhood. Cut the cake, hand her gifts and write down who they're from, make a toast and avoid in-depth conversations with everyone because today is not about you. Forget to eat anything because you don't have time, and the thought of food makes you gag. Be the perfect host and acknowledge those who helped you put such a fabulous event together.

When the guests leave, help the mom-to-be load the car with her gifts. When she stops for a moment to give you a hug and say thank you one more time, tell her you love her and are excited to meet the baby. Tell her with sincerity to call you if she needs anything. Be honest and let her know she can count on you as the day draws near. Smile so she believes you. After she leaves, walk back inside to finish cleaning and say goodbye to the rest of the guests. Pick up trash and tidy up with the help of the last guest: often an older woman. Maybe she's your tía, or your mother's comadre, an older cousin or [insert the name of a barren woman here]. She's someone who knows you or at least has heard of your futile attempts at conception. When you walk past her, she stops you, takes the plastic trash bag out of your hands and says, "I just wanted to tell you that I know. I know this was hard for you, but you are a beautiful and kind person for doing it anyway. I see you. I see what you did here. And I just wanted you to know that I know."

Try to smile and stay strong, but know that the game is over. She hugs you. Because there is no one else in the room, hug her back and let the smile in your eyes become tears.

❧ ❧ ❧

Maybe I am the one who needs mothering.

Rock-a-by baby
on the treetop,
when the wind blows
the cradle will rock.
When the bough breaks,
the cradle will fall,
and down will come baby
cradle and all

OPEN

after the doctor spread me open with the speculum
    & told me I would still not be a mother
I drove home in silence   after the storm

rubble lay on the road from the heavy winds
    & I felt autumn leaves falling
from the place inside me   where I used to believe

a tree full of mangoes could grow   ripe
    & succulent fruit drops & rots in my island cells
shedding each month   sour nectar

on the other side of a busy street   I see
    an open tree trunk   cracked like an egg
a black mouth agape, suspended in a scream

soft-braided bark stoned   by thick amber   molasses
    sap run dry   a sepulcro   for scorpions & ants
ash ground   fissured by drought   & seeds lay barren

like all the women torn   from the womb of motherhood
    the earth before the salt   the sea before the sunrise
the consequence of darkness   the water that never breaks

the tree begged me   to crawl   deep into its
    shadows   split open its sorrow   swallow
my skin & feed it   my red hysteria   inside its root

I pressed   against an exile of hollowed bodies   where poppies
    bleed instead of bloom   & jasmine
splinter the light   into a thousand whys

I waited for the folds   of my hands   to heal
    my womb to soil   & my body to be—
come but a breath   beneath the soil   (s)mothered

SHADES OF RED

THE FIRST TIME I wore red lipstick, I was twenty-seven. A few months after the miscarriage, Mami told me to get pretty. "Ponte bonita," she said. "Te vas a sentir mejor, ya verás." She believed wearing make-up and a cute outfit would make me feel better. So, I fumbled through earrings, faded jeans, worn-out clothes and shoes that didn't fit my swollen feet. I stopped to catch my breath between a sudden hot flash and a spontaneous dizzy spell. I wanted desperately for it to look effortless, but didn't know where to begin. I found a black top and black pants and black shoes and decided red lips and accessories would have to do.

※　※　※

Red lipstick is for cualquieras . . . whores. Women of the street. Mujeres de la calle. Red is a scandalous color. Not meant for proper señoritas and housewives.

Before twenty-seven, red frightened me. I was afraid of "el qué dirán," of what others would say. Of what Mami would say. Of what everyone would think. But eventually, I realized that if I was strong enough to survive the loss of a child in my womb, then I was woman enough to be dangerous. Woman enough to wear the color of blood and fire without fear and without trepidation.

※　※　※

I chose a cherry-red liner and a matte scarlet lipstick. Hands shaking, mouth stretched, I inched close to the mirror and began. Left to right, I drew in a line. Bottom lip first. Good. Top lip next. Okay. Then filled in the rest, like a child completing a color-by-number painting. I smiled. It smeared on my teeth. I sighed. Suddenly it felt like I should have a cigarette dangling from my mouth. I wiped my teeth and dabbed off the excess. I smiled again. Better. I took a picture. The room began to spin. I felt sick. My meds. Or my blood pressure or something else. I tried to smile. I tried to feel pretty. Lipstick smeared again on my teeth. I only felt objectified.

Despite the nagging voices in my head that told me it was too early in the day for red, that told me I looked trashy, that reminded me that lipstick wasn't a cure, I was determined to wear it out of the house. And I did. I wore it to the grocery store, and no one gave me dirty looks. I took a picture and flaunted it all over my social media. It stained my lips and refused to come off when I washed my face later that night. I almost didn't care. I wore it like the woman on the Sí se puede poster. Resilient and rebellious, I wore it as a sign of defiance against Mami's conservative nature and Papi's strict rules of order and tradition.

My Papi, a Latino military man whose main rules for me growing up included:

1. Do well in school . . . always.
2. No shaving or make-up until age fifteen.
3. No dating or boyfriends until age eighteen.
4. No sleepovers at anyone's house . . . ever.

I broke rule # 2 at thirteen, when I was tired of being bullied for my hairy legs. I often tricked Mami into letting me break rule #4, and in high school I regularly broke rule #3, but never got caught. If and when I did get caught breaking any of the other rules, Papi would react harshly and without remorse. One of those times involved red lipstick.

At the pre-pubescent age of ten, I walked out of the shower half-dressed and bumped into Papi in the upstairs hallway. I looked up at him and tried to scurry away so I could go to my room and get ready for bed. I was dripping wet, and it was cold in the hallway. He grabbed me by my arms.

"Look at me," he said.

"¿Qué? What? ¿Qué pasó?" I said trying to gently shake him off like the water that covered my small, shivering frame.

"Mírame, look at me."

I jerked my face in his direction and looked him squarely in the eye.

"Are you wearing lipstick?"

"No," I said earnestly.

"Let me see," he said as he put his thumb on my mouth and started rubbing my lips as if he were wiping dirt off the bottom of his combat boots.

"Papi, stop. I'm not wearing any lipstick."

I pulled away from him abruptly this time, trying not to drop my towel and lose the last shred of childhood decency I had left.

"Go show your mother." He needed more proof.

My soiled word and his clean thumb weren't enough.

"Dad, I'm not wearing any lipstick," I attempted to scream but my voice cracked, knowing I had already crossed the line.

"Go. Show. Your. Mother. Sonia!" he yelled across the house, "Mira a ver si esta hija tuya tiene los labios pintao."

"Papi, please."

"Vete. Ahora. I don't want to have to say it again."

The tears welled up. The one time I was actually innocent, I was still being punished. Truth was, it was winter in Tennessee and my lips were chapped. As a perfectionist, I had spent my time in the shower biting my lips raw. I hated the thought of my lips looking scabby. Between the heat and the cold and my lip-biting, my mouth had swollen up red like ripe strawberries.

I wanted to use what words I had left to stand up for myself, to prove that I had done nothing wrong. But because I feared Papi's strong arm more than I cared about my own weak pride at age ten, I walked begrudgingly to my parent's bedroom, where Mami lay in bed reading the Bible.

"Papi wants you to check that I'm not wearing lipstick." I awaited her judgment.

Mami looked me up and down. Unlike Papi, she didn't have to touch me to know my lips were clean. She was a woman. She knew the difference between chapped lips and make-up.

"Dile a tu papi que no joda," she said and looked back down at her Bible. She wanted me to tell Papi to fuck off.

Wide-eyed, I stared at Mami.

"Ma . . . " I shifted my weight, trying to stay warm.

"¡Ella no tiene na'! ¡Déjala tranquila!" she yelled across the house, then shooed me off with her hand and told me to go get ready for bed.

I left the room rubbing my lips and choking on rage. I went and put on my PJ. With sleep now only a distant memory, I decided to go to the living room where Papi was lying in his recliner, watching for the hundredth time *The Rise and Fall of the Third Reich* on the History Channel. He squinted as I walked past him to the other sofa.

Surveying me up and down like a drill sergeant during formation, he said, "¿Seguro que no tienes los labios pintao? You know you're not allowed to wear make-up yet."

"Yes, Papi. I'm sure."

"Don't let me catch you wearing any make-up. Tú sabes las reglas de esta casa."

"I know, Papi." I said while picking at the scab on my arm.

"Hand me the remote," he said after a few minutes. "Y vete a dormir. You have school in the morning."

I sulked for only a fraction of a second and, like a good girl, biting my lip and holding my tongue, I followed his orders and went to bed in silence.

᪥ ᪥ ᪥

I'm staring at myself in the mirror. The room is spinning and I'm hungry and I'm tired. I know that red is the color of blood and of love and of fear and of danger and of fire and of roses and of hearts and of my other organs and of apples and of womanhood. Womanhood. Womanhood. Oh, how I missed being a girl.

WAITING

THIS FERTILITY CLINIC SAT at the end of a narrow hallway on the seventh floor of an office building reserved for private practice doctors and specialists, such as reproductive endocrinologists. The double glass doors were heavy, and I always forgot whether I needed to push or pull. This always caused the awkwardness of my pushing or pulling a door that refused to open. The waiting room was not well lit. It was moody and dark like a hotel bar after sunset. I wondered if this was to empathize with their patient's moods, or if it was so we could hide our shame and grief.

It was a narrow room with comfortable armchairs and a plush loveseat adorned with decorative pillows. The porcelain lamps sat on end tables stacked with magazines that nobody read. There was a large mirror framed in mahogany wood on the wall behind the loveseat. It created the illusion that the room was bigger than what it was. In each corner, there were artificial plants that looked very real until you touched them. I believed the plants were there to convince us that we were in a fertile place where things could grow.

After I checked in and paid my $50 copay just to get blood drawn and pee in a cup, I sat down and looked around the room. That early morning I was one of six people in the room. I was there to begin treatment for my first round of IUI (intra-uterine insemination). I sat in the chair closest to the check-in desk and took out my phone, like everyone else.

Out of the corner of my eye, I noticed a dark-haired Asian man in khakis and a baby blue button-up. Next to him was a very petite woman in a wrap dress. Presumably married, they sat to my right

104

filling out forms. Based on the stack of papers they were filling out, I knew this was their first visit, the initial consultation that would take the longest time and likely end in the most tears. They would sit in the doctor's office, stare out at the city skyline to avoid eye contact and explain how they had tried and tried and tried on their own to get pregnant but couldn't. She or they would cry and hold each other's hands. The doctor would hand her a tissue and tell them that he would do everything he could to help them start a family, as if they were not one already. The woman would leave feeling hopeful. The man would feel relieved that his wife had hope.

The other couple across from me was Latino. I knew because the man, in a baseball cap, jeans and a Polo, spoke to the woman, with blond highlights and dark indigenous skin, in Spanish. They were not filling in any paperwork. When called, they went into the doctor's office and came back out in less than five minutes. I assumed they had come to get test results. As they walked out, I watched them leave and tried to read the woman's facial expressions. What were the results? Were they pregnant? What had happened in those five minutes? Was she okay? She noticed me staring and looked away as soon as we made eye contact. I didn't see a spark in her eye or a smile on either of their faces. I would never know what the doctor told them, but I hoped she was pregnant so she wouldn't have to come back anymore.

The other woman in the room sat alone on the loveseat. She had bags under her eyes, and her ponytail was coming undone. She wore yoga pants and a T-shirt for the Susan G. Komen Breast Cancer Walk. She looked like she had grown weary of waiting. I wondered if she was on her first IUI or IVF cycle or her fifth. Maybe the number of treatments would have made a difference in her appearance, maybe it wouldn't. Regardless, if she was here, it was because she, like I, couldn't do this on her own. That truth was tiresome enough.

I had been in many hospital and clinic waiting rooms over the last few years. Usually there was a television on, and patients often made small talk with each other. But in a fertility clinic waiting room, no one spoke. No one even bothered to look up at anyone else. We all looked down at our cell phones and hid the whites of our eyes to protect them, like eggs in a crate, afraid our fragile shells—fragile selves—would crack on contact. If we happened to look up, we made sure to stare at an inanimate object—the lamp or an artificial plant. No one besides the receptionist smiled or said hello. No one talked about the weather or traffic. No one wanted to be here.

Waiting at a fertility clinic was awkward. We all knew why we were there. The world had made us believe that we should be ashamed of that fact. The world didn't not treat infertility like the disease that it was. Instead, the world made us believe that somehow this was our fault. The world said this disease was not polite dinner conversation, and that as a Latina I should have had no problem getting pregnant and having babies. And the world expected that if we were brave enough to speak of our problems, then we should be required to answer questions about why and how and what next. The world also expected us to take unsolicited advice on how to treat, how to relax, how to adopt, how to pray and how to just "stop trying."

So, while we sat in the waiting room of the fertility clinic, we learned to stay silent. We let this silence fill the room and our wombs. We let this silence hold us because our stories were silenced. Silence did not need an explanation. Silence was the sound of sorrow and solace. Our silence was a moment of grace for our grieving bodies.

Because we were grieving, we chose to avoid small talk, or any talk that might've made all of this more real. Especially there, in this birth canal of a room, where we confronted the reflection of our own reality in the faces of all of those who waited—in silence—for our names to be called, for our turn with the doctor, for test results and telephone calls, for poking and prodding, injections and inseminations, for a live birth and a baby. We waited for the moment when we were no longer waiting.

PART III
SUMMER JASMIN(N)E

I will not survive
the flame tree
growing inside me.
Her blood swells
beneath my soil
& sucks the scent out
of my midnight lungs.
She's just as hungry
as I am.
Neither one of us
able to bear fruit.

GLUTTONY: UNDIGESTED

I am never enough.

The doctors swallow my face
their eyes like tar seeping
through the cracks of city pavements.

Skyscraper hospitals spoon
my reflection into glass & pour
me into the mouth of a waiting room.

A surgeon orders a CAT scan to
slice my heart—-arms—legs
into bite-size bits & p i e c e s

Medical machines gnaw
at my breasts & my back
salivating on scars of skin.

I stick two fingers down my throat.

What is there left to give?
A shadow lodged in the sternum. A reflux
of regret. A hole   in the trachea.

I gag.

Because it hurts.
Because I'm hollowed.
Because—

Survival is not enough.

HUNGER

Little *white* lies.
      We tell ourselves and each other little white lies all the time.
               I'm not black, I'm Dominican.
I feel fine.
I'm well.
               I'm not black, I'm Latina.
I don't care.
I don't want to get pregnant right now.
                   I'm happy.
                   I understand.
I'm just . . . tired, hungry, frustrated, sad, annoyed . . .
I feel fine.
               We're not "trying."
               I'm not black, I'm Hispanic.
It's just . . . heartburn, PMS, a stomach ache, a small headache, fatigue . . .
Yes,
I'm good.
                   I don't care.
I'm so happy for you.

Yes,
I have time.
                   I'm okay.
I'll go.
Yes, doctor,
I took my medicine.
                   I slept okay.
That feels fine.
Yes,
                   it's okay.
I'm okay.
                   It's fine.
Yes . . . yes . . .
                   yes . . . yes . . .

꙳ ꙳ ꙳

My day off began like all my other days off: with a doctor's appointment. I knew that this wouldn't be a routine visit to see Dr. Hassan, my rheumatologist, because I had been having some pain in my side, extreme fatigue and some shortness of breath. I had scheduled the appointment the day before, and I truly believed that I'd be in and out of his office with a new prescription in my pocket and a sense of relief by lunchtime. I skipped breakfast, saving my calories for a mid-morning waffle I had been craving for days and was certain I'd be able to enjoy once I handled this nuisance known as my "health." I threw on some clothes (and by that I really mean that slowly and gently I sat and clothed myself while I gasped for air) and drove myself to the doctor's. When I got there, they sent me to have a chest x-ray at an imaging center that was halfway around the medical center.

On the way to the imaging center, I stood in the street looking up at skyscrapers with names that promised healing and health. But I only felt suffocated. I stared at the map the nurse had given me to navigate the busy med center streets, tunnels, trains, bridges and parking garages. But as usual, I couldn't make sense of the lines and arrows or the compass and the key indicating north, east, south and west. I turned the paper left and looked right. I looked up at the street sign and held the paper up to the sun. I turned right and looked left. A car zoomed past and almost knocked me off my feet. I steadied myself on a light pole. By some miracle, the nurse who had sent me to get the x-ray had left the office for a few minutes to get a coffee. She saw me and was able to point me in the right direction.

When I arrived at the imaging center, I was relieved to know there would be a long wait. Finally, I could sit and rest. No more walking. No more catching my breath. No more dizzying people and sounds and sights and smells.

The x-ray got taken care of after many delays, and the lovely nurse came back to get me after the doctor told her he was concerned about my shortness of breath. Despite my objections, she kindly found me a wheelchair and pushed me back across the two and a half blocks to the doctor's office.

As I reflect now, I believe that being highly encouraged and almost forced to sit in a wheelchair was the beginning of my discontent. I was not incapacitated! I was only a little fatigued. I could walk with my own two feet; it would just take some time. Why couldn't anyone understand that, show some compassion and just slow down? I did not want to be made into an invalid. I just wanted to go to IHOP and eat a damn waffle.

I sulked and writhed inside. When we arrived at Dr. Hassan's office, they took my blood pressure (which was elevated), temperature, height and weight. I sat in the exam room impatiently waiting for him to tell me what I had, give me a pill and send me home. Dr. Hassan knocked gently and entered with a folder in his hand and a wide-eyed expression.

"I just got the x-ray results back. You have a pericardial effusion. That is, fluid around your heart. Your blood pressure is high, and I am concerned about your kidney function. We are admitting you to the ER right away."

What the hell?! I had no idea what was happening or why, but after a series of breathe-in, breathe-out stethoscope checks, a set of unrelated questions about my scleroderma and a phone call from the guy who reads the x-rays confirmed the diagnosis, I was back in a wheelchair being pushed to the ER. I had a doctor's note in my hand, an empty stomach and a heart full of fluid and rage.

❧ ❧ ❧

Within minutes of being admitted to the ER, five different health professionals entered the room and began poking and prodding me. One inept nurse tried to put in an IV and take my blood. She missed my vein several times. Another asked me to take off my clothes and put on a gown and another one attached probes for an EKG. An intern asked me questions about my general health, and a doctor tried to listen to my lungs amid all the chaos. I laughed and nervously wriggled in the bed, answering questions as I heard them, handing over an arm, a vein and a boob, breathing deeply in and out. I still didn't understand what was happening or why I was there.

I realized in that moment that I was no longer a human being with a soul. I was a human body with a problem, a cracked shell that needed mending, a scientific experiment. And I was finally "over" all of it.

This is stupid, I thought to myself, as residents and nurses and doctors buzzed around me. A curtain closed. Someone opened it. Machines beeped as frantically as everyone moved, and my stomach grumbled. You've got to be kidding me. I don't have time for this, and I'm so hungry I could eat my arm. My hunger morphed to rage. Who has time for these things? It's my day off, not a sick day, but a real legitimate day off. Why am I even here? Nothing really hurts, except for everything they're doing to me. This is absurd.

They ran more tests, drew more blood and extracted urine. After the first few hectic minutes, things calmed down. I had an echo done of my heart, which confirmed over 800 ccs of fluid and inflammation around the heart. The echo was so fascinating that the doctor grabbed two interns to show them. Great, I thought, how I ironic that I, a teacher on my day off, had officially become the lesson plan for the day. The two gentlemen beamed with excitement. They began to ask me questions I had already answered for someone else:

How old are you?

Where does it hurt?

When did it start?

What conditions do you have?

Is it okay to touch you here?

Can you lift your gown?

The only nurse who had bothered to learn my name must have seen the horror in my eyes as I stared at the interns. She had the compassion to ask me, "How are you doing, honey?"

I burst into tears. This, in turn, only pissed me off even more. I refused to let it have power over me. This was not how this was going to go down. Not today. Not anymore. Not ever again. I took as deep a breath as I could, stifled tears and stared at the needle in my arm. No one asked me anymore questions.

❧ ❧ ❧

Pericardial effusion/pericarditis, as explained by a doctor, is an abnormal accumulation of fluid and increased inflammation in the pericardial cavity of the heart, which can lead to impaired heart functioning. My definition of pericardial effusion/pericarditis was, stifling the tears and pain of a miscarriage, infertility and chronic illness for so long that your heart does the crying for you and begins to drown, because its tears have nowhere to go.

❧ ❧ ❧

Eventually, the ER doctor came in and explained to me the series of problems I was having. The human heart naturally has a little bit of fluid around it for protection. I, on the other hand, had a lot more. The theory is that this was probably caused by my scleroderma, or possibly lupus, and being off of my meds for so long in what had a become a futile effort to conceive and start a family. This is what is known as a "flare up." If the fluid isn't removed or reduced, it can lead to heart failure. However, I was also suffering from possible renal crisis. Renal crisis is kidney failure, which was also induced by my scleroderma, or possibly lupus, and was now elevating my blood pressure, which of course was also bad for my . . . heart. In conclusion:

1. They would have to give me drugs to reduce the inflammation and fluid around the heart, but . . .
2. Those drugs would elevate my blood pressure even more, sending me into renal crisis. So . . .
3. They had to give me other drugs to really lower my blood pressure in order to give me the heart meds. Or . . .
4. They would have to stick a needle in my heart to drain the fluid. Or . . .
5. Insert a tube into my chest and drain it out.

Those were my options. I was confused. I was livid. I just wanted a waffle. And yet, no one would feed me anything, "in case we need to prep you for surgery." In that moment, I decided that no one was going to cut me open simply because they wanted something to do. While everything was being explained to me, Lupe arrived and was updated on my status. We discussed what to do next. Luckily, Dr. Hassan, who had sent competent doctors to check on me, insisted on treating me with the drugs first. He wanted no probing, no tubes, no cutting. I trusted him, and I definitely did not want to be cut open or probed with a "large needle." We all agreed that that was going to be the plan. They would give me all the drugs they could to make this go away. I did not want or need to go under anesthesia.

I felt at ease for a moment. We had a plan. All would be well.

A few moments passed. Lupe squeezed my hand and asked what he could do to help.

"Can you find me a new body?" I asked without a hint of humor in my voice.

"I'd give you mine if I could," he said and held back the tears.

"Well, I'll settle for some food."

"I'll see what I can do."

He got up to try and buy me a snack from the vending machine, when a tall dark woman with long thick black hair thrust paperwork in front of my face.

"I need you to sign these forms."

I looked at her and then back at Lupe.

I shook my head in disgust. "I'm sorry, what is this for?" I asked, staring at the papers filled with medical and legal jargon written the size of sand grains.

"This is to consent for the pericardiocentesis," she said, tapping her foot impatiently.

I stared at her.

"The procedure to drain the fluid out of your heart," she said, clipping her words, her breath tense and impatient. "I need your consent so the cardiovascular surgeon can do the procedure."

She shook the papers in front of me and handed me a pen.

I crossed my arms, sat up in the bed and, with as much dignity and strength as I had left, I found the word I needed to finally start mending my own heart. "No," I said. "That's not happening. I'm not doing that."

Her face dropped. Her eyes searched me for an explanation, as if she were waiting for the punchline, or for the "just kidding" tone at the end of my statement. I knew she was not used to this type of rejection from patients—especially not from "critical" patients like me in the ER.

She shook the papers at me and then tried to hand them to Lupe, who only looked her up and down, surveying her bright blue scrubs, thick thighs and resolute posture, until she stood with the papers at her side exasperated.

"This is what the cardiologist recommends. You need to have this done," she insisted, shoving the papers in my face again.

I flapped them away like swatting at a nagging mosquito. "No. You or someone else needs to go talk to my rheumatologist. He and I agreed that I would not be having the procedure. They're going to treat me with steroids first. So, no, please go find him and figure it out."

I adjusted the itchy blanket on my legs and turned away from her to face the beeping machines and the sterile walls. I know you're not supposed to shoot the messenger, but I needed all these "specialists" to be on the same page about what was and was not going to be done to me. I had nothing left to say and, like a spoiled child, I refused to listen to any more of her bullying.

She stomped out of the room, swinging the curtain divider closed behind her, papers unsigned.

※ ※ ※

I spent five days in the heart and vascular intensive care unit, where they monitored every inch of me 24-hours a day. Five days of heavy steroid dosages, IV tubes, heart monitoring, blood pressure checks, all the waffles I wanted, friends and family coming and going, sponge baths and a lot of reality TV and magazines. And no one was allowed to cut me open. It almost felt like a vacation. I didn't get better and I didn't feel rested, at first, but the fluid and inflammation slowly began to diminish, and my strength returned. I don't give full credit to modern medicine for my slow but steady recovery. I believe it had more to do with the fact that I had finally said, "No." No to being controlled by men in white coats. No to following rules that let foreign objects penetrate my sacred spaces. No to being an object to be studied, to be colonized, to be worked on. I was more than just the sum of my broken parts for them to decide how to mend. I had finally decided to save myself.

INTERRUPTIONS

scrubs and sanitizer   x-rays and echoes   an EKG and an MRI
needles and nurses   poke and prod   blood draw   IV drips
cholesterol check   blood sugar pin pricks
a syringe in this arm   not the other   a history of illness   a record of pain
check   my weight   my height   my pulse   and my veins
open a curtain   a resident smiles   he can't spell my name   or my prescriptions
he finds me a blanket   asks   "How are you feeling   what brought you here?"
heart palpitations   shortness of breath   lupus   scleroderma   a pain in my chest
tells me to wait while I rest   it's a routine visit   turned hospital admittance

9:00 pm

check in

nurse knocks on the door   "Hello, how are you?   Tell me your name.
Is that how you spell it?"   shuffles around the bed and my face
"Yes,"   and   "Thank you,"   is all I have/time for
every 30 minutes   they swing open the door

9:30 pm

temperature check
steel under tongue   hand on my wrist   "How are you feeling?   Warm enough yet?"

10:00 pm

weight check
get on the scale   stumble to stand   fall to the floor
a tremble inside me   a fast-beating heart   washed ashore

11:00 pm

time check
I've tried to sleep   with one eye closed   and the other one listening

I guard my body   like jewels in a safe   don't want to be touched
don't want to be coddled   don't want to be   here

11:30 pm

shift change   "I'm the new nurse.   How are you feeling?   Why are you here?"
heart palpitations   shortness of breath   lupus   scleroderma   a pain in my chest
she looks at the chart   writes on the board   smiles at her
clipboard and walks out the door

MIDNIGHT

I trace the watercolor mural   of scrubs and shoes   in and out   blurred sight
fluff a pillow   rub their eyes   keep me up all night
burnt-coffee breath   and icy gloves   check my pulse "How are you feeling?"
"Where does it hurt?   On a scale of one to ten . . .   Why are you here?"

12:36 am

breathe in   breathe out   stuff my face in a pillow   and shout

1:00-4:00 am

coming and going   coming and going   machine beeps   IV drips
blood pressure check   and needle sticks

5 am

medication time
little paper cup   brought to the room   sit up in bed   swallow the pills
one red   one pink   one yellow   one blue
they tell me to rest   dull the sound in my chest

6 am

breakfast time   no sodium   no carbs   no sugar   no dairy
need to protect   my heart   and my kidneys

119

7:00 am

housekeeping comes   ammonia and bleach   filters the air
changes the sheets   empties the trash   meets my eyes with her stare
"¿Cómo te sientes?   Qué joven estás."   whispers a blessing   and I whisper a
"Sí"
roll over in bed   and try to sleep

LUPUS

A wolf bit the side of my face.
Her spit flooded my lungs
& hurricaned around my heart.
She howled at the soft moons
rising in my wrists & knees.
Echoed in my joints & swelled
between the gums of my teeth.
Chased me every night.
Ran me out of breath.
Slept inside my rib cage.
Pressed against my chest.
I tied her to my bedpost
& tried to feed her ginger.
She clawed at my marrow
& sucked the bone dry.
A wolf bit the side of my face.
The scar became a butterfly.

ER VISTS

I LIFTED MY SHIRT and pants and was hooked up to an EKG machine because I was once again in the ER complaining of chest pains and shortness of breath. The nurses asked for my health insurance card, and there began the usual flurry of activity I had come to expect in these cases of emergency.

Velcro ripped on the blood pressure machine, vitals checked, machines beeped, the paper curtain rustled open and closed behind me. I stood on the scale, answered inane questions and explained why the pulse ox-meter said I was not breathing.

"I have Raynaud's. You're not going to get an accurate reading from my fingers."

The young white female nurse in baby blue scrubs looked at me and said, "You're too pretty to be this sick."

I stared at the retro tiled floor annoyed by her comment. "Thank you, but clearly lupus doesn't care how pretty I am."

She smiled with her perfectly bright white teeth and continued placing leads on my ankles, chest and stomach. She asked me for my medical history. I recited my chronic diseases like the laundry list that they were. Lupus. Scleroderma. Raynaud's. Hypothyroidism. Hypertension. Pericarditis. Pericardial effusion. GERD.

She nodded, smiled again and walked to the other side of the bed to start the echo.

A second nurse, a burly black man in faded emerald green scrubs pulled the curtain open, picked up my chart from the edge of the bed and eyed me and my chart up and down.

"Do you suffer from anxiety?" he asked, skeptical of the young girl sitting on the edge of his ER bed with leads stuck to her chest and legs.

"No," I said and sighed heavily.

It was always the first question male nurses and male EMTs asked when I complained of chest pains. They seemed to have a hard time believing someone like me could suffer from chest pain that wasn't related to anxiety or psychosis. He leaned in close to me and listened to my chest with a cold stethoscope. He grabbed my wrist with his blue rubber-gloved hand and checked my pulse. His fingers on my wrist felt like soft chalky flesh, and he smelled of aftershave and day-old coffee. I wanted to vomit but had been asked not to move while they performed the echo test. So I swallowed the burning citric acid bubbling up from my esophagus and held my breath.

"Can you tell me about your medical history?" he asked, clearly not having paid attention to anything written in my chart.

I exhaled forcefully and recited my diseases again.

"And you say you've never suffered from anxiety?"

"No! My chest actually hurts because I actually have a history of heart problems."

He grunted, seemingly annoyed that I had raised my voice and said, "You're too young to have all these problems."

I sat up in the bed and leaned in toward him.

"No, actually I am not. Lupus predominantly affects black and Latina women of child-bearing age, young people like me. Medically speaking, I'm the perfect age for 'all of these problems.'" I knew I knew more about my disease than what he or most ER doctors and nurses had ever been taught in medical or nursing school, and I had just schooled him.

He stared at me, impressed and bewildered at how I knew so much about my own body.

"Do you work in the medical field?"

"No," I said impressed with myself, "but I am a teacher."

He continued the exam without asking me again if I suffered from anxiety.

"SICK" HUMOR

"IT IS SO GOOD TO SEE YOU out of the hospital! How'd it go?" asked Mary, my good friend, as I opened the door and let her into the house.

"Ugh, it was awful! I was there for three days and they had to change my IV five different times!"

Mary, a petite twenty-five-year-old with dirty blonde hair and bright blue eyes, hugged me and handed me a bottle of red wine. I had kicked Lupe out of the house for the evening and invited a few girlfriends over for a lady's night. Mary was the first to arrive, libations in hand. I put the bottle of wine down on the counter and stretched out my arms to show her my veins.

"I look like a heroine addict! Look at these bruises!"

We laughed, and she wrinkled her nose and shook her head in disgust. Mary also suffered from multiple auto-immune diseases and was all too familiar with hospital stays, bruised veins, incompetent medical staff and chronic pain.

"Girl, the last time I was hospitalized, I was there for two weeks! By day five I had been poked 12 times! I finally broke down and told them to call my doctor to get a PICC line in my chest, which is what they should've done in the first place!" She yanked at her neck collar and showed me the scar. I shook my head. PICC lines, or peripherally inserted central catheters, were used for long-term IV antibiotics and medications. Instead of a normal IV inserted into a small vein in the arm or leg, PICC lines were thin catheters inserted into a large vein, usually in the chest and meant to last days or weeks

124

at a time. They took a couple of hours to insert but did prevent multiple IV changes and needle pricks.

"The hospital nurses and doctors don't get it. Our skin bruises easily, and we are slow healers. They can't and shouldn't treat us the same as everyone else. If we tell them we need a PICC line from the beginning, they should believe us, instead of insisting on using a regular IV," I said as I uncorked the wine and served us each a glass.

Wine was technically off limits for me, given my relentless, high blood pressure and the fact that it caused the inflammation in my lungs to get worse. But I needed to relax and knew that I could spend the next day recovering if I needed to. I had just returned from my third hospital stay that year, because my recently diagnosed lupus was running rampant and attacking almost all of my organs. I had developed inflammation and fluid around my lungs, skin lesions that itched and scarred all over my body, high blood pressure, severe joint pain and swelling. To make matters worse, my Raynaud's was acting up and causing painful ulcers on my fingertips. Lupe had taken me to the ER one night because I couldn't catch my breath after dinner, and I was having severe chest pain. At the ER, they ran the usual round of tests, x-rays and CAT scans and decided to pump me full of steroids and keep me in observation for a couple of days until the inflammation in my heart and lungs calmed down. I was only there for three days but it had felt like weeks.

"So what was it this time?"

"It was my lungs and my heart. I couldn't breathe, and my chest hurt really bad. I thought for sure I was having a heart attack."

"Oh God, that's awful. I'm so sorry."

"It is what it is. I'm just glad to be home. Hospitals are the worst. Especially the people at the ER. When I told them I was having chest pain and couldn't breathe, the first thing they asked me was if I suffered from anxiety!"

"Oh my God! Yes! They did the same thing to me the last time I went. Like why can't they just believe us?"

"I don't know. I basically had to tell them my whole medical history with an oxygen mask on my face so they would believe me. Once I explained that I had lupus and pericarditis and used all their fancy medical words, they rushed me to the back and started running tests."

"I swear, we have more medical knowledge and expertise than the people who have spent at least a decade in school supposedly learning this stuff."

"I know. If I would've started medical school when I was first diagnosed, I'd be a doctor by now. And I practically am with everything I know."

"Cheers to that."

We laughed and clinked our glasses together. There was a certain level of cynicism that developed from living with a chronic illness that only people like Mary and me could truly appreciate and understand. We compared battle scars like soldiers at war because it helped us feel less alone. We tried to "out-sick" each other, not because it was cool, but because we had to share our stories to survive and to give each other hope that if we had made it through that, we would make it through this. We had both lost some of our "normal," healthy friends after diagnosis because young healthy people didn't understand what it meant to be sick. When we cancelled plans at the last minute because of a sudden flare up or fatigue, we were called flakes and unreliable. Our healthy friends didn't like being reminded of their own fragility when they looked at our hollowed cheeks and sunken eyes. Eventually, some of them stopped calling, inviting us out to dinner or the movies or sending get-well cards, because being our friend was too emotionally exhausting. It was too much work to find out if we were okay and to really listen to how we felt or what we were going through. Our previous friendships with healthy people usually became superficial. Small talk about the weather followed by a few well-intentioned "get better," "everything happens for a reason," "stay strong" and "God has a plan" platitudes failed to provide solace or comfort to anyone.

Mary and I were both diagnosed in our early twenties. Although I had been living with my diseases longer than Mary had, we had both been in and out of the hospital far too many times to count. Doctors didn't know what was wrong with Mary yet. They had originally diagnosed her with rheumatoid arthritis, until she started developing more complex issues, such as digestive problems, liver damage and mouth sores. I kept telling her it was lupus, but her doctors weren't convinced. She was losing more and more weight each day because she couldn't keep anything down. Despite the elaborate make-up and cute outfits she always forced herself to wear, I could tell she was not well. Her eyes were bloodshot, her skin looked yellowed and translucent and she walked really slow, as if every step she took required considerable effort and caused an immeasurable amount of pain.

Mary wasn't sick when I first met her. In fact, she was very healthy. She liked hiking and yoga and was always bubbly and energetic. We had met through a mutual friend and instantly hit it off. Less than a year after we met, she started developing symptoms. First it was joint pain, swelling and fatigue. Eventually she started having symptoms of inflammation and pain in other areas of her body: her skin, stomach and lungs.

I had been diagnosed for several years already when I met Mary and had always been open about my illnesses. When Mary's doctors couldn't figure out what was wrong with her, she started coming to me for advice. She asked me about my symptoms and medications, who my doctors were, what she should do for the pain, the fatigue, the frustration of not being able to do all the things she used to do. I always did my best to tell her what worked for me but always reminded her that everyone was different and that these diseases attacked everybody differently. She appreciated my honesty and told me I was the only friend she had that truly understood.

Mary wasn't the only chronically ill friend I had, but she was the first one I had met outside of a support group. I didn't usually hang out with any of the support group people because they all lived far away, were much older and sicker than me or had children and other responsibilities that kept them from having an active social life. It was nice to finally know someone my age that I could call or meet up with when we were both feeling strong enough.

That evening, though, I was really worried about her. I could tell she hadn't been sleeping well and the small sores on her nostrils looked painful and angry. The over-sized black tunic she wore hung

limply on her thin frame, and her collarbone jutted out from beneath
the neckline. I wanted to ask how she was doing, but I didn't want to
bring her down. We hadn't had enough wine yet to give in to crying.

In an attempt to keep the mood light, I said, "Well, the food at
the hospital was good at least."

Mary laughed, "What hospital were you at?"

We both knew that hospital food was usually bland, cold and
nothing to brag about.

"Memorial Hermann."

"Oh, yeah, their food is awesome."

"I had the turkey burger for like three days!"

"Yes, the turkey burger is good! I usually get the baked chick-
en."

"Oh, that's really good too. You know what I love most about it,
though?"

"What?"

"It's the fact that I don't have to cook it!"

Mary and I both laughed and clinked our glasses in agreement.

"You know what I hate most? That I can never get any real sleep
or rest at the hospital."

"Right?! Nurses and technicians and cleaning people and doctors coming in and out all night. . . . It's awful. And they're always
saying 'get some rest, try to sleep.' I would if they would just leave
me the hell alone for five minutes."

"For real."

"Oh, my God, you won't believe what happened to me this time.
Because I was getting pumped full of drugs with the IV, I had to drag
the stupid thing around any time I got up, right? Well because I
wasn't really bedridden, I refused a bedpan, 'cause that's the worst,
you know? Well, one of the times when I got up to go to the bathroom to pee, I somehow got my underwear tangled in the IV pole!"

"What?!" She squealed and started laughing.

"Girl, I don't even know how it happened. I just know my underwear was dangling from the IV tube and I couldn't figure out how to
get it off. I had to call Lupe into the bathroom with me, and he just
laughed at me for like 20 minutes."

"Did ya'll get it off?"

"Yeah, but I had to step over the tubes and spin around three times and unhook the IV bag. It was ridiculous."

We laughed some more and sighed. I took another sip of wine, groaned deeply and shook my head.

"This shit sucks, you know?"

"Yeah, I know," said Mary.

We fell silent. The dark comedy that was our lives suddenly didn't feel funny anymore. "So when do you have to see the doctor again?"

"I dunno, maybe next week I think."

She nodded and the doorbell rang. I got up and answered the door. It was my girlfriend Isabel. Isabel was in her late twenties like me. She was a peppy middle school teacher who loved outdoor sports, including white water rafting and mountain biking. She had short brown hair, olive skin and big brown eyes. She was petite and muscular and believed in clean eating, climbing the career ladder and feminism. She was generous and kind and was always checking in on me, even when I didn't call or message her back.

She and I hadn't been friends for long and still wasn't used to having someone chronically ill, like me, as a friend. My hospital stays, doctor's appointments and constant pain were new to her. She reacted to all my news of illness with extreme worry, but insisted that I was "strong" and "brave" and "heroic"—titles and accolades I didn't feel I deserved since all I was trying to do was stay alive. But she was the kind of person who had little experience with illness or death and couldn't understand how someone so young could be so sick. In her eyes, I was a superwoman for enduring so much.

"Oh, my God, how are you?!" She dropped her purse on the floor and gave me a hug.

"I'm good. How are you?"

"Worried about you. I saw your post on Facebook about being in the hospital again. I felt so bad I couldn't go to see you. I was so worried. Are you okay?"

"Yes. I'm fine. It was just the inflammation around my heart and lungs acting up. The doctors just wanted to make sure they got it under control early."

"Oh, my God, your heart and your lungs? That's so scary and so awful. I'm so sorry you had to go through that."

"It's fine. Really. I'm okay now. I'm on a ton of drugs, as usual, but I'm okay."

"Well, you look great! I'm so glad you're better." Her bright red lips smiled and she patted my shoulder.

Mary looked at me from across the room and smirked. She had friends like Isabel too. The kind of healthy friends who had good intentions but didn't really "get it," and never would unless they suddenly got diagnosed with a chronic illness too. I told Isabel I was fine and chose not to tell her what I really wanted to say which was that looking good did not mean I was "better." I didn't have the energy to explain yet again what chronic meant. Getting her to understand the humor in bruised veins, exposed breasts, bedpans and bad hospital food would have been futile. She would have laughed awkwardly and changed the subject because those kinds of conversations made people like Isabel uncomfortable. Isabel was the kind of person who needed me, her sick friend, to get better. In her mind, young people like me didn't get sick and almost die. Young people like her and me and Mary were healthy, invincible and strong. Sickness was a sign of weakness, and Isabel needed to believe that good health was guaranteed for the young, so she would not have to worry that this could happen to her. But the truth was it could happen to any of us. It was happening, and none of us were immune. I didn't want to have to explain to Isabel that being out of the hospital didn't mean I was cured, or well, or not in pain. So I told her I was fine and poured her a glass of wine.

Once Isabel started talking about work and her students, I knew that my conversation with Mary about frustrating hospital visits and imprudent nurses and doctors was over. I knew it wasn't polite or kind to talk about our intimate, albeit sometimes funny, experiences in front of healthy, optimistic and naïve people like Isabel because it would just make her feel bad. Because hospital stays were sad. Illness was sad. Chronic pain was sad. No one wanted to be at a girl's night feeling sad. I had also grown used to protecting other people's feelings with regard to my illness. I knew that just because Mary and I chose to find humor in our suffering, it didn't mean everyone else could or wanted to. People like Isabel didn't find illness and suffering funny, but that's because she didn't live with it on a daily basis like we did.

Even though the moment was over, and I knew Mary and I wouldn't be able to freely talk about ourselves the way we had before Isabel arrived. It was comforting to be able to laugh, even for just a moment, with someone who truly understood. If we couldn't laugh about it, what else were we supposed we do? Cry? Get angry? Scream? I knew that's what everyone else expected us to do, but we did enough of that already. We cried in our cars after a doctor's appointment. We shoved our head in a pillow and screamed until our voices cracked. We threw things across the room when our hands wouldn't work. We constantly felt sorry for ourselves and the lives we would no longer live. We carried sadness in our bones and anger in our lungs. Sadness was a side effect of loss. We learned to live with it and manage it, and sometimes the best way to do that was to laugh. And it was this laughter and this need for joy that made us brave, because it showed everyone, including ourselves, that we weren't afraid to keep living.

YOUNG, PRETTY & ABLE

I'm too young to be this sick.
I'm too pretty to be this tired.
I'm too able to have parked in that spot.

Witness: Invisibility—

Breasts & legs clothed   in hospital sheets.
Wrists & chest   laden   with tubes that leak salt water oceans
I may never see   again.

Witness: (Auto)Immunity—

Pulse ox-meter tattoos itself round my knuckles   timing
the tempo of a failing, fluid-filled heart.   EKG & MRI   measuring
the pericardial pentameter   pounds & pops in my chest.   I
almost had a stroke.

Witness: Infertility—

Tissue clots & clutters within.
Abdomen bends & breaks.   Life erupts   Blood cascades.
A flamboyán tree grows   rojo,   crimson,   barren   between
my legs.

Witness: Infection—

Gangrened fingertip.   Severed at the bone.   Hands hold on.
Fluid   hope &   concrete knobs.   Sewn at the tip.
Phalanges flail. Grasping at straws.

Witness: Inflammation—

Legs that stutter up the stairs.   Lungs that shudder.
Barometric pressure plummets.   Cold morning sinks
into crippled joints & bone.

Witness:

A body   bullied & beaten   without your words or weapons.

STROKE

BACK STROKE. Breaststroke. Brush stroke. Heart stroke. How many women die of a stroke each year? Why did it almost happen to me?

I pushed my feet off the concrete and flew. The chlorine bleach stung my eyes but I wanted to see where I was going. I wanted to feel the liquid breath that sustained me reach into every pore and fill me with life. I wanted so many things.

My doctor wanted me to do so many things. He wanted me to exercise, but I couldn't. He wanted me to stay active, but it was draining. He wanted me to find a workout I loved to do and to do it. So I swam.

Back stroke. Breaststroke. Brush stroke. Heart stroke. How many backstrokes would it take until I began to soar?

Swimming was the closest I would ever get to the liberating feeling of flying. I was a human, tethered to the ground by gravity and legs. But swimming made me feel weightless and free. Sitting in a plane was not the same as floating and flying through water. When I swam, I felt limitless and expansive.

Back stroke. Breaststroke. Brush stroke. Heart stroke. How many breaststrokes before I could finally breathe?

Three or four times a week I slathered on peanut-butter-thick sunscreen at SPF 80+ to avoid the excess sun exposure my doctors cautioned me against, went to the pool, ran weightless laps under water and swam. I could flip and turn with ease. I sank and rose. The water swelled and I didn't. My lungs ballooned against my rib cage and filled with air the way they couldn't when I was on dry land. My

134

muscles expanded and flexed, my joints slithered instead of stiffening and the cracks in my skin softened like warmed clay. When I broke bread with the pool, I flew back into myself and out of the world. I was not anchored to my illness or pain, to my diagnosis or my dreams deferred. It was the only time I could remember "normal."

MOUTH SORES

I'm learning to grow a garden
inside the mouth of a volcano.
An asteroid of red planets
crashes inside my cherry
cheeks. A hard palate
depression burns red A feast
of flames feeds on my gums
brands the roof of my mouth a
full moon crater. I chew
on poppy seeds until my teeth
bleed & amapolas flower my
tongue. I swallow amaryllis
tissue until it blossoms in my
throat, I pluck its petals from
a scream. Hibiscus springs wild
from my lips & I learn to suck
the nectar out of sorrow.

MO(U)RNING MEDICATIONS

sticky feet scoot   soot across the floor   morning light   empties night

kitchen sink   release a gauze of water faucet hiss   fills the hourglass

seven rows   split in two   purple day   green night   the barrel of a gun

before the pull   scheduled rounds unloaded   these pills

stand their ground   suppress what the body won't   quell the bone sigh   whisper

inside me   it's trigger time   pop   a prayer   pop   a black widow
boat-tail pop   a bronze full-metal jacket   pop   a round nose   self-defense
bullet   pop

the slow release   of fire in the body   a groan gruel   stomach grumble

a gag   a gurgle   pink blood   pressure spits   white memory ashes

blue capsule backfires   lavender gas   swirls in my nostrils   mint thyroid reset

half-cocked remedies   swallow me slow   into ~~remission~~ submission

DETOURS

EARLY ON IN OUR RELATIONSHIP, Lupe and I learned that we loved to take road trips. He would always drive and I usually fell asleep. But when I was awake, we often played games: "20 questions" or "What if." These were the kinds of games that helped us learn a lot about each other and also led to arguments. We would ask each other hypothetical questions about how to raise our future kids or what we would do during an apocalypse. I learned, for example, that Lupe would probably leave me to die during a zombie attack because I would not have the energy to fight, and he would not have the desire to carry me or fight for me.

When we were traveling to somewhere new, I was responsible for managing the GPS system. Lupe knew I was terrible with directions but trusted me anyway. Inevitably, we got lost and had to make at least one U-turn on the way. I called these moments "adventures." Lupe never found our detours and turnarounds fun, in the way I tried to, but he learned to expect them and deal with them with patience and calm. I didn't mind getting lost on the road with Lupe because I trusted he would get us to our destination. Sometimes we discovered new places together or back roads that helped us arrive at our destination sooner. When that happened, he agreed that it was quite an "adventure."

I never drove on road trips or even locally if Lupe was around. Most of the medication I was on warned me against it, and Lupe hated my driving skills, anyway. I even hated to drive short distances around town and avoided it at all costs. Sometimes, however, I needed to run errands or go to a doctor's appointment in the middle of the day, when Lupe was at work.

One morning I had to drive my overly medicated self to my rheumatologist's office for a follow-up visit. I decided to take back roads to get there because, although I knew the freeway was faster, I did not trust myself on the busy Houston highways. The warning on one of my medications, prednisone, warned against operating heavy machinery until I knew how the drug would affect me. That morning, the prednisone was in full effect.

The corticosteroid prednisone, one of the worst drugs I was ever prescribed, turned me into a forgetful, insomniac, overweight nightmare. High doses of prednisone made me insufferable to everyone, but especially Lupe. I was irritable and angry most of the time and would often snap at him over the smallest things: "Stop breathing so hard" or "Why are you chewing so loudly?" The drug itself was intended to reduce the inflammation in my body, but it wasn't meant as a cure or a long-term solution. The side effects of prednisone were many, and it was risky to take for an extended period of time. Long-term prednisone use could lead to cataracts, osteoporosis, Vitamin D deficiency and a host of other irreversible problems. It was, nevertheless, the only drug that gave me the strength and energy to work, clean the house, write and have a social life. I loved prednisone and hated it all at the same time.

I never knew how prednisone would affect me from one day to the next. That morning, it made me feel drugged. My face was tingly and going numb around the cheeks, and my head felt like it was under water. My eyes had a hard time focusing and my hands trembled. While driving, it was hard to focus on street signs, I had zero patience for slow drivers and found myself zoning out while at a stop sign and forgetting to cross the intersection. I knew it wasn't safe for me to be behind the wheel, but I had to get to my appointment. If I didn't, it would take another three months to get in to see the doctor. I didn't want to be on this much prednisone for another three months.

As I made my way to the doctor's that morning, all the back roads I knew so well started to look the same. I started feeling anxious. I clenched my jaw and began to grind my teeth. I narrowed my eyes to try to make sense of the road and the buildings around me. My heart began to pound. The farther away from home I drove, the foggier my thoughts became. I opened the window to let some air in to see if the breeze would help me refocus, but it didn't. It still felt like there was a cloud of gray smoke in front of my eyes and I had just fallen off a merry-go-round.

After a number of turns and stops, I realized that I was sitting at a stoplight completely lost. I looked left. I looked right. I saw tall buildings all around me. Trees lined the pavement. Cars and people crossed the street. I didn't know where I was. The street sign said Fannin. I recognized the name. I had been on that street dozens of times before, but could not remember how to get to my doctor's office from there. I didn't even remember how I had ended up there. I remembered leaving my house, getting in the car, making a few turns and suddenly I was at this stoplight. Of all the side effects of prednisone, this was the scariest. This was brain fog. And there was nothing I could do to make it go away. I sat in my car with the wind blowing on my face, lost and confused.

I started to panic. Someone honked at me. Shit. Where was I? They honked again. I started to drive, but my hands shook. I could feel my heart beating faster, my breath becoming shallow. I looked left. I looked right. Nothing looked familiar. I rubbed my eyes, thinking that maybe I just wasn't seeing the street signs clearly. That didn't help. I looked around again and noticed there was a parking lot two blocks away. I decided to stop there and call Lupe.

"Amo. Lupe. I don't know where I am." My voice shook and I was yelling.

"Slow down. What do you mean? Where are you?"

"I don't know! I was on my way to the doctor's, and now I'm lost."

"Okay, just hold on. Look around you. Is downtown to your north or to your south?"

"What?! I don't know! What do you mean?"

"Look out the window, where is downtown, to your north or south? You'll want to drive away from downtown to get your doctor's. Where is downtown?"

"How the hell am I supposed to know? I was on Fannin. Now I'm in a parking lot. I don't even see downtown."

The skyscrapers of the medical center blocked my view of everything. I gripped the phone, unbuckled my seatbelt and frantically turned side to side in my seat to look for downtown. I leaned my head out of the window, but still couldn't find it. I knew that I probably looked as crazy as I felt. I felt seasick. It was like my mind had left my body and floated along without me. I could still feel and see my body and everything around me, but I didn't have the words or the logic to make sense of it.

"Please don't yell at me. I'm just trying to help," said Lupe in a calming way that seemed to irritate me even more.

"I know. But I don't know where the hell I am, and you're telling me to drive away from something I can't even see." I started to cry.

"It's okay, baby. We'll figure it out. Just look out the window and tell me what you do see."

"Um, the med center, I think. Texas Methodist maybe?"

"All right. You're close. Put me on speaker, set the phone down and drive out of the parking lot." I did as he said. "Now, is Texas Methodist to your east or west?"

"What the fuck, Lupe?! I don't know what that means!" I cried harder.

He sighed trying to find the patience to deal with me. "Is it to your left or right?"

"It's in front of me!"

I wanted to throw the phone out the window. Lupe was not helping and I was ready to give up, go home and spend the rest of the day under the covers, where it was safe.

Lupe was not willing to give up on me. "Just breathe, honey. Go ahead and turn left and get to Sunset Blvd. You'll have to turn right and that will take you back into the med center where your doctor's office is."

I drove in silence for a few minutes, both of us too frustrated to engage in small talk.

After a few moments, Lupe asked, "You there? You see it?"

"Yes." I looked up at the building where my doctor's office was located and suddenly everything came into focus. I knew where I was and I recognized my surroundings.

"Do you know where you are now?"

"Yes. Thank you. I'm sorry I yelled at you. I just freaked out. I didn't know where I was. It was scary."

"I know. Don't worry. It's an 'adventure!'" he said, mocking me. I couldn't help but giggle a little. "This was not fun."

"I know. But you're fine now. Call me after your appointment so I can make sure you're good to drive home."

"I will. Love you."

"Love you too. Be careful."

I made it to my doctor's appointment that morning because of Lupe. Without him, I probably would've sat in that parking lot, cried for an hour and missed my appointment. Every day and in every way, Lupe was my compass and my guide. I may have held the GPS when we traveled on road trips together, but he helped me make sense of all the roads in life that diverged and twisted and turned and took us on uncomfortable dark journeys we thought would never end. When I felt afraid or unsure about what to do next in life or where to go, he held my hand and led the way with confidence. Whether we were on a road trip to Louisiana or San Antonio, or off to find a new restaurant in town, he sat behind the wheel and got us there despite my poor directions. And whether we were trying to navigate through infertility treatment options, buying a house or changing my medication, he always pointed us in the right direction and got us back on track. Even if we ended up somewhere completely different from where we had planned, he always made it clear that he felt lucky enough to have me on the journey with him. After all, getting lost with someone was always a more exciting adventure than traveling alone.

INFLAMMATION

I.

I try to swallow el calor with a glass of prayer
        beads & for years it sears my stomach a hole.
An untreated ulcer scathing the gut. Heartburn.
        Indigestion. Inflammation dwelling in the membrane
of my melanin. Smoked-swollen joints billow the size
        of volcanic rocks. Embered. I carry too much
heat in my body.

II.

Is it el o la calor? I ask Mami in the Texas
        summer heat. Blanketed by shade, she says
the heat can be either or.

My native Spanish tongue drags & stumbles
        between el o la, la o el always trying
not to cross an artificial border without the right papers.
        El calor, I say, when it hacks at my skin,
a slaughter of cells, the Dominican guardia wielding
        machetes & damming the river life lines under my skin.
La calor, I say, when it blows damp, an ocean breeze
        ready to mother my wounds & heal heat sores
scabbing over stained-glass sweat.

El o la I fumble & fall into a hole filled
        with the flesh of words I am still acquiring
a taste for. Dulces palabritas from home.
        Words that feed my lips childhood stories of people
pinned to walls above altars lit with sage smoke
        & candle wax. La o el tourniquet that stops the flow
of words from resting in my mouth like water.

III.

"Este calor me va a matar," Mami says & I linger
        in summer sun memories bubbling with questions
& self-doubt. Again I ask, "Is it el o la calor?" She simmers
        and says, "Just remember, el calor, la calor, is fluid.
Like our blood. Like your Spanglish. Like our bodies
        across our borders should be."

HEART

"MAMI, can you hand me that, eso, esa cosa over there," I said, pointing to a broom with my index finger.

I needed to sweep the living room. Dog hair was everywhere, and dirt and dust, all made me feel itchy. I needed her to get it for me because I was already out of breath from folding clothes. I wanted that thing across the room, but I could not remember what the thing was called.

I was still on high doses of prednisone for my lupus. I had energy, or at least a false sense of it, and I needed to get things done, but my body was moving faster than my brain and my words just couldn't catch up to a mouth that spoke before it even knew what it was ready to say.

"¿El qué? What?" she asked, looking back and forth at my finger and the pantry and speaking to me in English. After 30 years in the United States, she finally felt confident enough to speak it with me.

"The . . . the . . . ¡Tú sabes! ¡Eso!"

My hands flapped like a bird whose wings had been set on fire. I could not think of the word in English or in Spanish, and my legs weighed heavy as if I had been wading through oil or mud all morning. The lupus-induced inflammation that made my ankles swell the size of mangos left me little to no desire to take the 50-foot walk across the room to get it.

Mami walked over to me and placed her palm on my shoulder and, with a tender but demanding touch, sat me down on the couch.

"Ya, sit down. What are you trying to do? Te vas a cansar. Sit down," she said, shaking her brown head of hair rolled up in curlers. I imagined this was how she used to speak to the four-year-olds she taught in pre-school before retiring to spend her days taking care of me. And because I resented being treated like a child, I got back up and tried to move past her. But she stood tall and relaxed, staring me down, like a Dominican guachimán sworn to protect the entrance of a five-star resort filled with gringos.

"Please, Ma. The floor. It's dirty," I finally was able to spit out, gesticulating at the floor and rubbing my nose to indicate that the dust bunnies and clusters of dog hair were irritating and unacceptable.

I pointed again across the room to the broom. Like playing a game of unsuccessful charades, I pantomimed sweeping the floor. Her feet remained planted in front of the couch, unmoved by my pleas.

I was relentless. "Quiero the . . . the . . . eso," I said, pointing. "¿Cómo se llama?"

Mami frowned. "¿La escoba?" She pointed to the white-handled broom with wild yellow bristles leaning against the pantry door.

"Sí. Yes. Eso." I plopped down on the couch, fatigued, and sighed with relief because she had figured it out.

"No, you're not going to sweep. You can't even breathe. Siéntate. Yo lo hago."

"Ma, I feel fine." I got up, coughed, caught my breath and wiped my brow.

"No. Antes nunca querías limpiar. Y ahora que no puedes . . ." She shook her head. "Siéntate." It was not a request or a suggestion. It was Mami's definitive "or-else" kind of "No."

So I sat back down.

She was right. I hated doing chores as a kid. Mami used to have to force me out of bed on Saturday mornings by turning up the merengue music on the boom box, entering my room with the roaring Rainbow vacuum cleaner and pulling the covers off of me, so I'd help clean the house. I'd moan and groan every time, stomp my feet and complain how it wasn't fair. Mami would roll her eyes, hand me a wad of paper towels and a bottle of Windex or furniture polish and tell me to get to work. I'd dust every nook and cranny. I'd wipe down all the knickknacks, the fans, the banisters, the decorative mirrors, the coffee table, the bookshelves (of which there were many because my father was a well-read man) and the entertainment center. My Saturday mornings were rarely spent in front of the TV or outside with friends. Saturday mornings were for cleaning, and I hated every minute of it.

After my diagnosis, however, I'd been unable to hold a full-time job. Because even such simple activities as showering, getting dressed and brushing my teeth were exhausting. Doing chores and keeping my home neat and clean were the only tasks that made me feel useful. On the days that I could cook, clean and sweep, I felt like I was not just the sum of my broken parts. I was not just an ailing body waiting to get worse. I had some purpose, and being a mediocre housewife was better than being bed-ridden.

I sighed at the irony of it all as Mami brought me a glass of water. As she swept the dirt and dog hair from under my feet, I relented, having lost this battle. So I sat on the couch, repeating escoba, broom, escoba, broom, escoba, broom, so I would never forget those words again.

❧ ❧ ❧

I speak English. I speak Spanish. I can read music. Essentially, I know three different languages, but in those days, my English and Spanish words would get jumbled in my mind before they were uttered by my mouth. With the steroid meds that accelerated my thoughts on an endless repetitive loop, the lupus fog that blurred and clouded my mind and the endless litany of "more important" medical things I needed to remember, it seemed that I had even forgotten the lyrics to some of my favorite songs in both English and Spanish. I could bop my head to the rhythms, but I could not get the words out. I hummed along with the Caribbean trumpets and saxophones when Juan Luis Guerra's merengues played, and every once in a while I'd get a line in the chorus right. I'd belt it out—"¡Buscando visa para un sueño!"—until I felt the bass in my skull and the treble vibrate my chest. And then I'd start to cry. I could not control it. A melancholic bachata love song played, and my eyes would water. An upbeat Celia Cruz salsa of leaving the island for a better life or a Calle 13 cumbia hip-hop song about returning to the motherland played, and I'd find myself weeping like a hurt child. I was vulnerable to the familiar sounds, even if my mind could not make sense of the lyrics.

Growing up, whenever we couldn't find something, Papi would always say, "Búscalo en tu mente, está en tu mente," as if we could conjure the missing object up with our thoughts. But I wasn't missing a physical object. I hadn't misplaced my keys or my shoes or my credit card. I had lost my language. I could not make sense of my thoughts, could not find the words I needed because I didn't know where I had put them. I searched the valleys of my mind for simple phrases, like "I'm tired" or "Estoy cansada." All I could hear was the screeching rubber tires across the pavement of chronic fatigue. Why had the meds and the illness forced my words to migrate? Where, in this now colonized cranial space, could I find them? Why did I have to give up the melodies of my English and Spanish native tongues to make room for the language of science and medicine? When would this cat and mouse word game finally end?

During a recent visit, my cardiologist handed me the latest results to my EKG exam. I stared down at the print out and noticed how the jagged lines formed steep mountains and deep valleys, moving up and down, that blurred on the page. I didn't care to make sense of those hieroglyphics—they were just lines that measured the flow of blood and the strength of my heart. I did not want to be able to read the language of internal organ beats and half steps. The language of a life lived with chronic illness was not something I wanted to adapt to. I did not want to let this hostile vocabulary hijack my story. A story made of sipping coconut-rum drinks, merengues on the beach, rapping poetic island hip-hop and reggaeton with my friends from New York, dancing and singing upbeat salsas in the kitchen with Lupe and crooning love-sick bachatas with Papi in the car.

This medical jargon felt convoluted and cold, like the house music Lupe liked that made the room spin and the lights flicker. It felt synthesized and voiced-over and lacked blood and muscle and beat. I did not want to be able to translate these rugged edges and disproportionate angles on carbon paper. I did not want to converse with ease about systemic, anti-inflammatory, immuno-suppressive this or that. I wanted to hum along to the elongated tender vowels of my childhood Spanish and English, or bop my head to rudimentary nostalgic melodies of my middle-school-band saxophone. I looked at my cardiologist silently and waited for him to translate the lines into English or Spanish, or into the music or lyrics I could understand.

He said my heart beats like an uneven metronome. Tachycardia. My breath was short. Pericarditis. My blood pressure crescendos. Hypertension.

I heard his words echo around the room. I felt the silent beat of a heart in my ears. I stared down at the sharp peaks and valleys on the page. I let the page come into focus and I followed his finger as he traced the lines across the page, indicating what the highs and lows meant. I tried to keep from understanding, but I knew that I already knew too much. I wanted to refuse these syllables and accents but I was already fluent in too many of its words and their origins: scleroderma . . . sclero (hard)-derma (skin) . . . hard skin; -itis (inflammation) . . . pericarditis (inflammation of the pericardia (heart lining); pleuritis . . . inflammation of the pleury (lungs). But where was my body? Where was I in these words? What of this belonged to me?

The last six years, I had come to understand that all medical language, for the sake of both doctors and patients, must remain detached from its subject. The fingers that sometimes helped me function and sometimes caused me pain were not fingers; they were "digits." My mind, the one that I feared losing, was not a mind or even a brain; it was a "cerebrum." My body, attacking itself out of fear or hatred or whatever traumatic experience I couldn't seem to let go of, was "auto-immunity." This life of limitless pain and eternal illness was called "chronic." These linguistic distinctions allowed doctors to treat the illness and its symptoms rather than the patient. To them, I was tissue and bones, organs and cells. My body was not a container for my inner light or divine soul, as both Mami and I would've liked to believe. To doctors, my body was the subject of study, a problem they did not yet have an answer for.

No matter that I didn't want to learn this new language. I had been immersed in it by force. My mind had already learned to decode such phrases as, "Patient presents with reduced pulmonary function due to early signs of lung fibrosis and pleurisy in a CT scan." Or such questions as, "Is your scleroderma diffuse or systemic?" I knew I needed to know what these words meant in order to survive the world of the chronically ill and to communicate with all the "ologists" and specialists I interacted with on an almost daily basis. I had to prove to them that I knew enough about their world so they could see me and hear me and not just focus on the cacophony of sounds emanating from my broken parts. Yet, the more I assimilated into their world, the more desperate I became to hold onto the language that defined mine.

I was losing the words, the music and the memories from the languages that mattered to me. Although I loved both English and Spanish, because I lived in the United States, I was inundated with English television, English music, English lab results, English medical records and English pharmacy warning labels. Inevitably, my English continued to grow and seemed easier to remember. But it was my Spanish tongue and my Spanish ear for new words and old sayings that I was always chasing, always trying to resuscitate and always hoping to catch.

It was Mami's musical accents when she called me on the phone for the third time in one day to ask, "¿Cómo sigues?" or her ritualistic blessing, "Dios te bendiga," that assured me I wasn't alone. It was Papi's weekly instructions in Spanglish that began with, "Tu único propósito en la vida es . . . " to take my meds or pay my bills or llamar a la gente del seguro, that kept my to-do lists in order when the brain fog made me forget where I'd misplaced the scrap of paper I'd written everything down on. These languages shaped my memories. I needed my Spanish and my English to remember me, the me I was before.

So as I listened to the cardiologist explain what the rhythms beating beneath my chest meant, I knew that, more than anything, it was

Lupe's insistence on playing corridos on road trips and the sound of his teacher voice calling me Amo every morning and every night that reminded me that I was a Dominican-American woman who married a Mexican-American man, and we loved in both English and Spanish, and therefore mi español was a language—a song—my pericardium/mi corazón/my heart cannot afford to forget.

PART IV: WINTER JASMIN(N)E

in the heart of winter
buttercup bulbs erupt
& honey the air
a symphony of yellow

AVALANCHE II

What started as a hangnail drilled a hole in
the earth of my skin & bone until it found ice & snow.
The cold morning hit my hands an avalanche
I didn't have the gloves for.

Split fingertips slipped on slopes & drowned
in dry ice. I scratched at the tomato paste wound
     & blood that crusted on the nail and sloshed a muddy
brown until it waxed black and lost its warmth.

I whispered into the gangrened well of sores & scraped
black dahlia's from its walls. I tried to tip to grip a pen
     & fold my palms in prayer but my severed seaweed
dreams never did come true.

I let the surgeon cleave the cuticle, sand my joints & stitch
     my skin with sutures to dull the sound of leaving.

HANDS: EL CORTE

MISSING FINGERTIPS. Missing children. Missing papers. Missing legs. Missing women. Missing limbs. Missing lives. Missing each other. Missing the point.

"*Tijera colorada, tijera colorada*," erupted like erratic bullets from the mouths of Haitians, as language became their only weapon against machete blows of hate, fear and greed. Trujillo's men were ordered to spare no one.

Scleroderma has not spared me. A red scissor, *una tijera colorada*, was used to cut the bandage off my surgically severed fingertip. I watched as the nurse meticulously unraveled the gauze, asking, "Are you all right?" at irregular intervals while I gripped the chair and stared down at the cold sterile floor—the final step to what had been a grueling six months of wash, rinse, wrap and repeat.

This was the second time my poor right-hand third digit had had to go under the knife. Once before, they tried to remove the gangrened mess that had sored and festered for months underneath my fingernail, but the virus had invaded the bone.

You have to clear the infection before you can close the wound.

And the Haitian population insatiably grew like sugar cane stalks that were strong and proud, but easy to cut down.

"*Purificar la raza*," he said. "Cleanse the island," he said. In 1937, Haitians were alive and awake in the Dominican Republic when Trujillo's men hacked them to pieces along a river that had run red with blood once before.

156

Purple. Blue. White. Green. Black. But never red. It never turned red again. My finger failed to flow with blood, so it turned black instead.

Black. Too black. Those Haitians. *Son negros.* Dominicanos are mestizos, mulatos, taínos and españoles. It's in the way we speak. It's in the way we walk. We carry it in our blood. We feel it in our bones.

Before going under the knife, I had tested positive on a mandatory pregnancy test, and they warned me of the risks. Missing brain cells. Missing toes. Missing fetus.

If the soldiers gave you the perejil test, and you couldn't roll your "r's" just so, you would be one of the missing.

They drugged me slightly, but I was lucid. I was awake. They were awake. Awake enough to hear everything.

The crude jokes made by the nurses. Like the terrified screams heard along El Río Masacre. My hand surgeon's heavy breathing stifled by a mask, his echoing refrain to "Just relax" trickling from his lips as if it were Beethoven's Ninth Symphony, did nothing to make me feel joy. And the women and children cried and wailed, a requiem for the transnational island that would never be. The dead can't sing, but the wind could not stifle their piercing cries.

I heard the sawing and scraping of bone along a blade. Back and forth. Back and forth. They heard the crackle of plantain leaves and dry dirt crush beneath their feet as they ran and ran. And with the placement of every surgical instrument clanking and clinking on sterile stainless steel, I knew there was nowhere I could go. But I wanted desperately to get out.

Awake enough to feel a lot of pressure, like a tooth extraction, on my hand. Decapitated, axed and thrown into ditches. It was genocide. Where would the pieces of me end up?

Awake enough to feel the coolness of the metal table along my spine, I tried not to shiver for fear the doctor would miss his mark. The sweat glistened on their black bodies beneath the moonlight as they dodged and ducked the blades of bigotry swinging away at them.

Awake enough, we all held our breaths and said a prayer to a God we didn't think was listening.

Awake enough to know that when it was over, we would no longer be whole. We would always be broken.

Because fingertips, like people, don't grow back.

El Corte is when we cut down trees, we cut down lives, we cut down pieces of us and each other we no longer want and think no longer need. Until we miss them.

Month after month, my doctors and I cleansed the wound and waited for it to heal and close on its own, but it never did. I saw a hand surgeon. A rheumatologist. A wound care specialist, a physical therapist, a "therapist" therapist.

Trujillo was a dictator, comparable, some say, to Hitler. For seven days and seven nights, soldiers chopped and cut human flesh and bone until he was satisfied. Afterwards, they were said to have gone mad. Mumbling in the night. Sobbing in their sleep. Spiders crawling beneath their skin.

We all live in the quiet spaces that exist between acceptance and denial.

I spent six months on at least four different kinds of antibiotics and too much Aleve and Vicodin. My chronic pain was becoming a cliché.

More than 2,000 ethnic Haitians were able to escape along the border. Some even lived to tell their stories.

Remedies that weren't enough.

I wrapped and rewrapped the open sore every morning and every night with pink, purple and zebra printed gauze and tape, just to keep me distracted from the ugliness that hid beneath the surface.

I underwent 24 straight days of hyperbaric chamber oxygen treatments because someone had told me it had worked for them and saved their foot. Seven thousand dollars later, there was still a gaping hole where the tip of my middle finger used to be.

Witnesses say Trujillo had kissed a Haitian flag and recognized his Haitian ancestry, just months before the massacre.

Dominicans were given a 24-hour notice to leave Dajabón before the soldiers came. There is not an accurate count of how many Haitians were killed. Some say 12,000, others say 30.

My body and the island would not find the strength and capacity to heal themselves.

In a last ditch effort to save my sanity from any more suffering, I did what you do with anything you think you no longer need. I got rid of it. Like Trujillo wanted to get rid of them.

Amputees and refugees. Getting rid of things we think we no longer need. Until we miss them.

I went back into surgery to chop the damn thing off for good. It's just a fingertip, I thought. I still have nine more.

Trujillo said he would "fix it." Fix the Haitian problem, and "remedy the situation" in order to help Dominicans "enjoy in peace the product of their labor."

I labored to save this finger. I wanted nothing more than to be at peace. Let go of that which no longer served me.

I had lived through pericarditis and near heart failure, lung fibrosis and shortness of breath, chronic pain all over my body, extreme fatigue, two years of infertility, lupus skin rashes, high blood pressure in my brain and a miscarriage. A partial finger amputation seemed irrelevant. Until I missed it.

A gross miscarriage of justice. Some Dominicans claimed Haitians were stealing from them: taking land and cattle, shipping arms across the border. La guardia used machetes, bayonets and clubs instead of their government-issued guns so the government would not get blamed. It was Trujillo's first step towards "Dominicanization," but it didn't work.

The pregnancy test turned out to be a false positive. The Haitian Massacre did not eliminate Haitians from the border or the rest of the Dominican Republic.

So what was the point?

I will always feel the phantom pains of what once was there. An itchy fingernail. A desire to scratch what cannot grow back. The tingling, the trembling and my tip-to-grip capacity will never be the same. I got rid of the pain, but its memory still remains.

I realized I could never be whole until I'd been broken and put back together again in order to study the scars, remember the loss and miss it.

I am still chronically ill. Anti-Haitianism is alive and well.

A new ulcer has begun to form on the fourth digit of my right hand and it's refusing to heal. I'm not as eager to start cutting this time.

MORIR SOÑANDO

I had a dream once:

My machete hands slice open
calcified white green caña.

I milk my tongue into a glass
of homemade morir soñando.Watch it
roll into "r's" colorado, singing: perejil, perejil.

Lash my sun-kissed lips with sugar
to sweeten this café con leche skin.
Paint my pupil with the pulp of a banilejo mango
and bathe in seawater singing: perejil, perejil.

Cave into the earth that surrounds me.
Fill my flesh with fango. Swallow
the sounds of the island and bloom
from the bones buried beneath. Wake up
wounded. Wake up singing: perejil, perejil.

❧ ❧ ❧

Cutting cane for the general:

Stalks of severed limbs lay bare.
Sea foam spills from veins.

Machetes hack at wounded flesh.
Fill breath to the brim with salt.
Bathe the earth in sangre—

Set the field on fire.
Fire to harvest the cane.
Fire to flower the flamboyán.
Fire the scent of parsley.

Fire the sound of blade
hitting bone hitting body—
Fire 'til it swallowed me
crimson. Fire 'till I die
while dreaming.

HAIR

MY PATERNAL GRANDMOTHER had "selective eyesight." She had cataracts in her right eye and glaucoma in both. By all accounts, she was legally and medically blind. I learned, however, that there were certain things she chose to see or not see. Abuela, or Doña Basilia as her own grown children and my mother called her, was in her eighties. A dark-skinned Dominican woman, she preferred to deny the African and probably Haitian blood coursing through her veins. And she believed in the power of relaxers, cocoa butter and mani/pedis to make herself beautiful. She worked diligently in the DR and for some time in the United States to raise and provide for her six children (at one time seven, but one died of childhood diseases) all by herself. In order to help her family survive and thrive, she became hard and stubborn against the world. She was not the kind to say, "I love you" or "I'm sorry." Everyone in the family understood and accepted this about her, and we expected nothing more and nothing less than her critical eye and antagonistic sarcasm. After raising her family, she spent her old age in Florida watching telenovelas and celebrity gossip news on the Spanish channel until she had to bathe and change from one pink and purple floral bathrobe into another.

Once, Mami and I had to travel to Orlando for a funeral. I had to stand in for Papi, who could not take the days off from work as a school administrator. It was almost the end of the school year, and he was needed on campus every day. My abuela has never believed that Mami was good enough for Papi. When they first immigrated to the United States and Papi had to leave for basic training after enlisting in the Army, Abuela made my mother's life miserable. She'd always make snide comments about Mami's family being too poor and not educated enough, this despite the fact that Mami and Papi were neighbors and grew up in the same barrio. Mami says she never really defended herself against Abuela, because you had to respect elders: "Hay que respetar a los viejos." Mami never wanted to offend my grandmother by pointing out that they were just as poor as she was. Because she'd lived "under Abuela's roof" at the time, she knew anything she said in her own defense would be taken as a sign of disrespect.

Abuela always judged and belittled Mami by saying that her children were the darkest of all the grandchildren. The darkest con "pelo malo," bad hair, as Latinos like to say. Because we take our cues from European colonizers, in Dominican culture status and beauty are perceived in terms of skin color and "good hair," that is, European hair. The lighter the skin tone and the straighter the hair, the more "refined" and beautiful you are. The darker the skin and the coarser the hair, the more othered and ostracized you become. Despite the fact that Abuela herself was clearly a woman of African descent, she criticized the fact that my siblings and I were born as dark as we were. I suppose she had hoped that because Mami's own skin tone favored Spanish blood, it would help wash out Papi's melanin a little and save us all the trouble of being born black.

When Mami and I entered Abuela's humid home in Orlando that May, the air inside was moist and sticky. Nothing had changed since the last time I had been there, four years earlier. The same coconut-brown couch and recliners set up against the peach-colored walls. The same beige carpet and floral Home Interiors art work on the walls. The TV was blaring in Spanish and the fans spun uncontrollably.

Abuela peered at me from above her thick pink lenses.

I said, "Hi."

She squinted, furrowed her brow and snickered, "Oh, ¿y ésta quién es? ¿Yamina o Jenni?"

Mami emphatically asserted, "Es Yamina."

"Oh," Abuela said again and she chuckled, her shoulders moving up and down beneath her housedress.

I moved to her and gave her a kiss on the cheek, my lips painted her face with pink gooey lip-gloss. She smelled of fabric softener and magnolias. Her skin was soft and fallen, warm to the touch. As usual, I didn't feel any affection. I set my purse down on the dining table meant for a family of eight in a home that was only inhabited by one. I headed to the bathroom.

In the living room, the "Primer Impacto" TV show was humming in the background as Mami chatted with Abuela. I was trying not to listen, but the house was so small and the walls so thin, I could hear everything.

"¿Y cómo está Yamina?" Abuela asked.

I paused at the question. How was I doing? I wondered as I stared at my amputated fingertip and swollen hands. Mami assured her I was fine and that my health was "improving."

I sat there staring at my hands while I peed. I felt bad that Mami had to lie. Lupus was kicking my ass. I had recently developed fluid around my lungs after the stress of the partial amputation. My doctor was also concerned about possible kidney involvement. None of this was a sign of "improvement."

"Ah, qué bueno," Grandma said.

There was a pause, and I heard the voice of Walter Mercado on the TV, preparing to deliver our daily horoscopes. I tried to listen for mine.

Abuela continued prodding: "Pero, y ese pelo, ¿ya ella no se peina?"

What was I planning to do with my hair, she asked. It always came back to my hair or my weight. Did I not plan on fixing it? Didn't I comb it anymore—what happened? I sighed and shook my head. My hair had been natural for years. Thirty years in this country, and Abuela still carried her childhood and the weight of Trujillo's dictatorship on her shoulders. The burden of believing that white is right, that our café con leche or mahogany-colored skin and naturally curly or kinky locks weren't good enough . . . She still expected us to relax, flat iron, straighten, whiten, cut and kill every root and representation of our black side.

Mami laughed it off. "Le gusta natural. Es el estilo ahora." She explained to Abuela that it was easier for me to manage it this way, with the way my hands were.

But Abuela persisted, saying that it seemed like straight hair would be easier to manage, that natural "is just so nappy."

Mami snapped back, coming to my defense. "She likes it better this way. It's easier for her and her hands. And I think it's healthy and beautiful."

Although Mami had struggled with both my sister's and my hair transition, she had come to appreciate it and was proud of us for embracing so fearlessly what she was taught to reject.

There was no response from Abuela. What more could she say? I reasoned that she had decided to fight less and listen more in her old age.

I flushed the toilet, proud of Mami's subtle but necessary jab. I stared at my reflection in the mirror, touched my hair with my hands and heard Walter Mercado on the TV sign off with his usual catchphrase wishing the viewers lots of love, "Les deseo mucha paz, salud, dinero y sobre todo mucho mucho mucho amor."

MASSAGE ENVY

A BLIND MAN gave me a massage the other day. He stood over me, tall and sturdy like a linebacker. His burgundy, well-pressed scrubs hung loose on his wide frame, and he didn't need a cane to walk through the massage parlor's halls or to show me to my room. He knew this place well. He told me his blindness would not affect the quality of his work. He was right.

He left the room and I undressed. The dim lighting made it hard to see, and I wondered if this is how blindness begins. I felt a chill rush past my toes from the crack underneath the door. My skin tingled cold. The room smelled of lavender and rose petals. My other senses were now on high alert. I hurried myself onto the heated massage table to shelter myself from the chill air. It calmed me to know that this six-foot commanding man would not be able to see my stretch marks and biopsy scars. But I knew that our emotions manifest themselves in the body, and I wondered if he would be able to feel things in my skin, in my soft tissue, in my brittle bones that the seeing world could not. Would the warmth of my bones reveal years of repressed trauma and self-hate? Would my hard-to-knead thickened skin explain the walls I had built to protect myself against the world?

I shivered and tried to release the tension in my hips and butt. He knocked on the door. I clenched my jaw as he and the cold hallway air drifted in. I pressed my face into the opening on the table and stared at the purple carpet beneath me. He asked me if I was comfortable. I said yes. He asked me why I was getting a massage. I said I suffered from chronic illness and needed to learn how to relax. "Stress kills," I said, and tried to chuckle. He wrote something on his clipboard and said, "Okay." I heard him pump lotion into his hands

167

before placing them on my naked back. His marshmallow-like fingertips pressed tenderly between my left shoulder blade and spine. He rolled his knuckles down each one of my vertebrae as I tried to imagine what his hands could see: stubbornness braided along my back, fear pulsing angry red inflammation into my joints, a history of grief manifested as lung disease.

He asked if there was any place on my body he should be extra careful with or not touch. I asked him to stay away from my right hand because I was battling a non-healing wound on my finger. I said I had already lost one fingertip to a bone infection and I was trying to save another. He put more lotion on his hands, moved to the other side of the table and asked if I was diabetic. I said no. I said I have lupus and scleroderma. He worked my right bicep like a mound of raw dough and said he didn't know lupus could do that. I said, "Yeah, it can." He stroked my arm with the length of his fingers and said, "Bless your heart, what a shame." His tone and touch rushed over me warm, like cinnamon tea. He had said, "Bless your heart" and "What a shame" in that sweet southern way that is not condescending or pitiful, it's just the truth.

He is right, I thought. It is a shame that I cannot do some of the things I used to do, like write pen to paper, eat with chopsticks or lift myself up in downward dog during yoga. It is a shame that I have lost the use of 60 percent of my right dominant hand and have trouble brushing my teeth, combing my hair and feeding myself. It is a shame that every time I look at my right hand, I am reminded of loss.

When I first walked into the massage parlor and realized my masseuse was blind, I thought for sure I should feel sorry for him. But the truth was I only ended up feeling sorry for myself.

I clenched my buttocks as he palmed my sacrum and repeated, "It's okay, it's okay." He smoothed out my shame and sorrow the way one might smooth out the wrinkles in a flat white sheet. I finally let go, closed my eyes, and let the room go dark. He shadowed over me for the next 30 minutes, while my breasts, thighs, stomach and collarbone pressed achingly into the heated table. He opened my skin with his hands, his fingertips reaching into the crevices of me that my own hands could no longer reach.

DROP IT

I have lost the use of sixty percent of my right dominant hand.
So I d
    r
       o
          p
              things.

Things I need. Things I don't. Cups.
                  Plates.   Pens.   Bottles.
Paper.
    Bags.   Shoes.   Plates.   Fork.
        Keys.
Clothes.   Hangers.   Spoon.
    Toothbrush.   Pens.   Paper.

    Keys.   Pencils.   Earrings.

    Comb.   Bags.   Necklace.   Shoes.
I d
    r
       o
          p   things.
I rage.
I relax.

I keep d
r
o
p
p
i
n
g   things.   Pots.   Pans.
My phone.   Gloves.   Chopsticks.
    My wallet.   Keys.   Pills.   Knives.

        Plates.   Books.   Cups.   Phone.
I sigh   I d
            r
            o
            p   more things.
Sometimes they   b   r   e   a   k.
Sometimes I b   e   a   k.

        Lupe is always there to   pick up the p i e c e s.

AFTER THE AVALANCHE

I pull larimar & winter jasmine
from my flower bud fingertips,
warm the blue & the yellow
between my hands & harvest
a field of green.

PART V: TRUE JASMIN(N)E

I opened my mouth
to sing and scent
the stars
with my breath.
But howled
at the moon instead.

HOPE

MAMI HAS ALWAYS BELIEVED that there was nothing Papá Dios and a good meal couldn't fix. Mami was born and raised a Catholic, and so was I. I was baptized at the age of four. I received Holy Communion in the first grade at age seven. I went to Mass almost every Sunday with my family until I was old enough to have a legitimate reason to stay home, such as studying for a test. I was confirmed my sophomore year of high school at 15, and I was married at 24 in the Catholic Church by a priest. I had only been to confession four times in my entire life, but I knew how to pray using the Rosary, when to stand, sit, kneel and repeat during Mass. I'd even read the scriptures during service a handful of times. I was tied to the Catholic Church, even if I didn't believe in or follow all the rules. Mami applied her "Papá Dios" and a hot meal beliefs to my illness. Every chance she got, she filled me with sancocho and prayer. Whenever I heard good news from my doctor, she would seal it with a "gracias a Dios" or a "bendito sea Dios," followed by a "¿Qué quieres que te haga de comer?" or a "No te descuides con la comida."

Mami believed so reverently in the power of the Good Book and Jesus that she subjected me to several healing rituals, Catholic or not. On several occasions, "for the sake of my health," she put her staunch Catholicism aside and subjected me to "healers" and "spiritualists." She asked my tías and cousins to submit petitions to Sunday Mass. She prayed the Rosary every morning and, after my near heart failure and chronic lung problems, she even encouraged me to sign up for and receive the anointing of the sick.

I wasn't sure I wanted or even needed the anointing of the sick, since that rite was usually reserved for people on their deathbed. Recently, a local church had been offering the rite to chronically ill people. I wasn't feeling particularly religious or faithful nor did I expect to be miraculously healed, but I felt I needed something: spiritual peace, renewed faith or, at the very least, hope. I felt I needed the light to shine on or inside of me somehow. I needed to believe that all of my suffering had meant something or would mean something someday.

I signed up to receive the sacrament. The week before the ceremony, one of the parishioners gave me a book to read about the purpose of the anointing and what I could expect. I read it and felt even more certain that I needed the anointing. I was not physically near my time of death, but parts of me were long gone. I needed to do something to let them rest in peace.

I arrived at the sunlit, stained-glass church early and spent 15 minutes praying on my knees before the service began. The church was quiet and cold. A few other parishioners had also arrived early and were kneeling in prayer as well. Mami and Papi came into town to be there with me. Mami prayed a Rosary while we waited for Mass to begin. I could tell Mami and Papi felt at peace and were grateful I had not completely lost my faith. I knew they were hopeful this would help me somehow, even if I was still unsure. I still believed in something, I needed to, but I wasn't entirely certain this was it. I, nevertheless, had to try. I had to keep looking.

When Mass began and they asked those of us receiving the anointing to come up to the altar, I eased my way down the aisle, catching my breath and holding on to the pews as I felt the stares of the congregation piercing through my back. I imagined they asked themselves what I was doing there. What could possibly be wrong with such a pretty young girl? I wanted to turn around and sit back down and resign myself to the darkness. I couldn't bear to look at Mami's face and see the disappointment she carried in her eyes almost all the time now, so I stood in line with the others and waited.

The priest raised his arms above our bowed heads and began to utter words about "His holy anointing" and "His love and mercy" and "with the grace of the Holy Spirit." He then came to each of us and made the sign of the cross on our foreheads and hands with an oily substance. I exhaled when his warm fingers touched my wrists, but I didn't see the light. I noticed that my legs still hurt. The room began to shake in my peripheral vision. I swallowed hard, but my throat was dry and it got caught. I smelled incense. The room began to spin faster. I was not used to standing this long. My head pulsed and I needed to sit down. My meds were kicking in and I hadn't eaten breakfast that morning. I tried to steady my eyes and my feet to keep from falling over. I tried to pray, but the words wouldn't come. I thought for sure I would pass out right then and there.

The priest said a final amen and we all turned around. I blinked hard to keep my balance and bring the room back into focus. I looked up and saw Mami. She was smiling at me with tears in her eyes. Had she seen the light I hadn't? What did she know or believe that I didn't? She kept smiling as I walked towards my seat. I sat down next to her, and she put her warm hand on my thigh and said, "Te quiero." I was thankful the sacrament had worked for one of us.

✵ ✵ ✵

We were back in Florida and standing in my cousin's living room when it began. The evangelical Christian women in long skirts and dark tops sipped their hot Bustelo coffee, wiped tears from each other's eyes and read Bible verses to ease their afflicted souls. They were mourning the death of my uncle who had recently died from a sudden heart attack. While they prayed and bemoaned their loss, I sat in a corner on the couch reading emails on my phone. I had shed enough tears for everyone, including myself recently, and my spirit was tired. All I wanted was a distraction, and although my phone provided that for me, it didn't last very long.

From one moment to the next, before I knew what was happening, my three cousins, their mothers and Mami pulled me off the couch, grabbed hold of my hands and made me stand in a prayer circle. We bowed our heads. I kept my eyes open and stared at our toes. I wondered if they felt hot in their long skirts on that warm July afternoon in Orlando? A petite older woman with salt and pepper hair in a jean skirt and black blouse began to pray.

"Señor . . . Señor . . . Señor . . . ," she said over and over like the gong of a church bell that beckoned and demanded God and all others around to listen. "Oramos por esta joven, Señor. Bendita sea, Señor, que la sanes. Señor, bendita sea, Señor, estamos contigo Señor. Enséñale tu luz a esta joven, Señor. Que se cure con tu misericordia, Señor."

I realized what was happening. I had been forced into a healing prayer circle. These women were asking God for a miracle to cure me of my disease. Or were they doing it to stifle their grief and focus on what they thought they could control? My uncle was dead. They were not capable of bringing him back to life, but perhaps they gained comfort from believing that they could somehow help save me from the pain of illness and disease. They had just buried a man they really loved, and perhaps being close to someone like me, who seemed so close to death all the time, was so unsettling and ominous that praying over my body felt necessary.

As they prayed and squeezed my hands tighter and tighter, my palms began to sweat. I stared at painted and unpainted toenails and admired my cousin's Grecian inspired sandals. I wondered where she had bought them. I considered asking her later, after this healing prayer circle, but considered it would be rude to ask her about shoes when she was mourning the loss of her father. The women prayed an Our Father first in English, then in Spanish. I repeated a few of the words with them, but my stomach grumbled and I realized I hadn't eaten since the night before. The funeral service had been early that morning, and all I had had time for were my meds and a glass of orange juice. Why did I keep forgetting to eat before these things? Of course, I had no idea that today was going to become about me instead of the man we had just buried. I felt unprepared and was ready for lunch or at least a snack.

"Él te sanará," said the older woman again.

Mami squeezed my hand. She wanted me to be healed. I wanted to be healed, but I didn't think this was how it was going to happen. Everyone kept their eyes closed. I stared at Mami's toes. She needed a pedicure. I decided I would take her when we got back to Texas. Mami had been through a lot these last few years, dealing with me and with the loss of her siblings. She deserved to be pampered. She had suffered enough—we all had.

My stomach grumbled again. The women said amen, amen, amen. The lights in the room flickered and it felt like I saw little stars flash before my eyes. I closed my eyes and tried to focus. I didn't think this was the kind of "light" I was supposed to be seeing or experiencing. My hunger was making me cross-eyed and delirious. I wanted to raise my head and look around for food. I had to eat soon, I thought to myself. But was it polite to ask for food in the same place where a man had fallen to his death only five days earlier? I didn't think it was, so I kept my head bowed and decided I would wait for someone to offer me food. After all, this was a Dominican wake, and I knew someone would eventually hand me a plate and probably another prayer.

⚜ ⚜ ⚜

The next time Mami coerced me into participating in a religious healing experience was when she and Papi insisted Lupe and I have dinner at my Mormon uncle's house. Being Mormon in a mostly Catholic family was a huge oddity. Of course, we nicknamed him "the Mormon uncle." When both Lupe and I hesitated at the thought of having dinner with my super religious uncle, Mami and Papi told us it was just going to be a nice family dinner. But the truth was, my uncle had invited his "hermanos" from the Church of Latter Day Saints to give me a laying on of hands in order to "heal" me and release me from my sickness.

My uncle, a mild mannered, quiet but non-religious man for most of his life, had recently converted from Catholicism to Mormonism. Mami believed it was because he had recently undergone open-heart surgery and had probably seen Jesus, in all his divine light, calling his name. I considered it was because the Mormons had come knocking on his door one Saturday morning, promising salvation and a peaceful afterlife, and he was too nice to turn them away.

Whatever the reason, he now went to a Mormon church and attended Book of Mormon study sessions on a weekly basis.

The night we went over for dinner, Lupe, Mami, Papi and I were joined by my uncle, his wife, his two teenage daughters and two young men from the church. I wasn't expecting anyone but my uncle and his family to be there, so I was taken aback by their presence. Both men were dressed in black pants, a white shirt and brown loafers. They had perfectly gelled comb-overs with a side part, bright white teeth and glasses. They came in smiling and carrying what looked like black Bibles and a stack of pamphlets.

When I noticed the pamphlets, I nudged Lupe wide-eyed and murmured between my teeth, "Dear God. I hope they're not going to try and convert us. I just want to eat. I only came here for the food."

"Did you know they were coming?"

"No. I swear I had no idea."

We walked to the dining room where the table was already set. After a few brief introductions, we all sat down to eat. The dinner went relatively well. My aunt had made a hearty Dominican dinner of stewed beef, red beans and rice, potato salad and fried plantains. We prayed before the meal, and one of the young men from the church even told a corny "dad" joke. As dinner was ending, I stood up to help my aunt clear the table.

"No. Siéntate. You don't need to help. This dinner is for you."

She took the stack of plates out of my hand, and I sat back down next to Lupe. I shrugged, unaware that this dinner had been organized "for me." My aunt left for the kitchen, her daughters trailing behind with cups and silverware. That's when the inquisition began.

"So, what exactly is wrong with you?" asked Tom, one of the "hermanos" from the church.

"Oh," I paused, not prepared to answer such an invasive question from a stranger. "Well, I was diagnosed with scleroderma a few years ago, and recently was diagnosed with lupus," I said, starting to get choked up.

"How does it make you feel?" asked John, the other "hermano."

"Um. I don't know . . . " I blurted out and my voice cracked.

Lupe put his arm around my shoulder. I could see from the corner of my eye that he too was uncomfortable with their line of questioning.

"What I mean is, where does it hurt?" asked John.

"Everywhere," I said, wishing that one word could pierce his flesh and cut him deep.

"Have you found God yet?" asked Tom as he reached his soft, unworked hands across the table towards mine.

I pulled my hand back and grabbed Lupe's under the table.

"Yes. Yes she has, thank you," said Lupe. He was getting angry. He had not spoken up before then because he wanted to respect the fact that we were in my uncle's home, but he knew that each question was making me more and more upset.

I had never minded talking about my disease before, but usually that was on my terms. I wanted to be in control of everything related to my illness—my narrative of it was all I had. I resented my uncle for telling these strangers I was sick. I resented these men for presuming they could "fix" me. There was something about having complete strangers accost me with questions and judgment that unsettled me deeply. Their tone made it seem like somehow my illness was my fault for not "believing" enough. I didn't need their scrutiny or judgment. I carried enough self-imposed guilt already. I hated them for their savior complex and for making me feel less than.

Suddenly the two men and my uncle stood up and picked up their Bibles or Books of Mormon or whatever they were. They walked over to my side of the table, and John opened his book to somewhere in the middle.

"Is it okay if we place our hands on your head?" asked Tom as he gestured what looked like angel wings over the crown of my head.

I turned for a moment to look at Lupe, hoping he would step in to save me. But then I met Mami's hopeful smile and Papi's smiling eyes and knew I couldn't say no. I had to do this for them. They needed this hope more than I needed my rage or my pride. I bowed my head as the two "hermanos" and my uncle hovered over me with their hands on my scalp and began to pray.

"May she be healed," said Tom.

"May she be free from sin," said John.

"May Your Almighty grace fill her and deliver her from this evil," they said together.

And on and on it went for about three minutes. I kept my head bowed. I cried. I had eaten too much. I was so upset I wanted to vomit. Food crept up my esophagus, and I grunted a few times during their prayers to keep it down. They prayed over me, and Lupe held my hand tight.

When it was over, I didn't feel clean, or holy, or healed. I felt used and tired. I took a long drink of water and wiped my face. I was so relieved when they removed their hands from my head. Their laying on of hands had given them power over me. I wanted to take it back but didn't know how. I had lost control of my own body and my own healing once again. I didn't want my life or my health to be in anyone else's hands. I was not anyone else's problem to fix. I knew then that my body and spirit weren't broken, just tired. That night, I washed my hair and scrubbed my scalp until I no longer felt any shame. I vowed to find a way to heal myself.

⅜ ⅜ ⅜

My yoga teacher, Rhia, taught me to tolerate discomfort. She taught me to breathe through it, accept that in yoga, like in life, this too would pass. She was a thin, short-haired blond woman in her early thirties like me, and she was passionate about yoga. Always encouraging me to come to class, she taught me how to work within my limits. She made me believe that my body was still strong, despite its flaws, and she made me feel like I wouldn't be sick forever.

Initially, we started with 45 minute private sessions she offered me free-of-charge because she knew how much I was hurting physically and emotionally. I had known Rhia from before I'd gotten sick and taken a few of her classes. After I expressed interest in beginning a steady and consistent yoga practice, she offered to give me private sessions to start.

During our workouts, she often pushed down on my joints with gentle ease and reminded me to let go and just be. I was comforted by her thin warm hands and lavender-smelling skin. As we worked on forward folds, modified pigeon poses and twists, she taught me that holding tension in my hips meant there was something I was refusing to let go of in my body and mind. When I felt comfortable enough to take a regular class with other people, we mediated on finding and restoring balance. We sat in silence in her yoga studio until I felt comforted and holy. She asked me to set intentions for each class and allowed me to be in control. For almost two years, I went to class weekly, meditated daily and went to yoga workshops and retreats, like it was my new religion. I listened only to my body and what it needed. I replaced all the amens I'd heard with ohms instead. Yoga helped me realize that I could pray when I wanted to talk to God and meditate when I needed to listen to Him. For a long time, with Rhia's help and guidance, I stopped talking to and at God and found the time to listen.

One day, after an emotionally and physically exhausting week of doctor's appointments, fighting with the insurance company, new meds and not enough sleep, I went to class to find the silence. When I walked in, Rhia could already sense that I was not in a good place.

"How's it going, friend?" she asked as she checked me in.

"Eh, it's been a long week. I'm tired, you know . . . of all of it." I almost began to cry but blinked away the tears.

"Oh, honey, I know. But I'm glad you're here. You made it, and that's all that matters." She smiled her perky yoga-teacher smile and told me to grab two blocks and a bolster. "This class will be just what you need. It's going to be really restorative today."

"Okay. I make no promises on how I'll do. I may just fold into a child's pose the entire time and fall asleep. But I'll try."

"You do what you need to do. This is your time."

She shook her bangs out of her face and checked in the next guest. I grabbed two blocks and a bolster and headed into the studio. I liked Rhia's studio because there weren't any mirrors there like at other studios. She didn't want her students staring at themselves and worrying about what they "looked" like while practicing yoga. She really wanted us to focus on our practice and to listen to our bodies.

I laid out my mat and lied down. I took a few deep breaths and set an intention for the day. I decided I would focus on being still. I would let my thoughts drift away and try to quiet my mind. Rhia came in and started class. It was a Yin Yoga class, which meant we were going to hold each pose long and focus on hip openers. My hips felt tight and achey, so I knew this was what my body needed.

After a 55-minute class of sun salutations, pigeon, double pigeon, lunges, twists, back bends, an inversion and feeling like I would die at any minute, we finally got into our final Shavasana resting pose. I breathed in deeply. Rhia walked around the room asking us to think about the intentions we had set at the beginning of class. She told us to thank our bodies for getting us there that day. She told us to be thankful for our practice and to know that where we were was exactly where we needed to be.

In those 55 minutes of class, I had been able to let go and be still. My mind didn't race with thoughts of pain or death or fear or fatigue. I focused on the poses and my breath. I was in control of what my body did or didn't do during class. I was not healed or cured, but I felt alive and calm.

Rhia came by my mat, bent down and rubbed my shoulders until they finished relaxing. My eyes were closed, but the room seemed brighter suddenly. She asked us to roll to one side, keep our eyes closed, sit up and place our hands in prayer pose in front of our hearts.

"Take one more deep breath in through your nose and out through your mouth," Rhia said. And we did. "The divine light in me honors the divine light in you, Namaste."

"Namaste," we all replied.

I took a deep breath, bowed my head and smiled. I realized then what I should have known all along: I didn't need to find the light because I *was* the light.

(W)HOLE

What is the skin anyway, but . . .

a graveyard for bullets, needles, blades & hands,

a map where lunar islands rise from follicles & blood,

a river of stained wood over gum muscle & vein,

a horizon of rolling amber hills laid over bone,

a web of collagen collecting the spiders of time,

a turtle shell coating tissue & tendon,

a honeycomb hole for ghost cells & iron breath,

a fishnet catching sunlight, dirt & slurs,

a canvas of fissured scars wrinkled with laughter,

a porous sponge emptying the gift of water,

a stained-glass window reflecting light to the world,

a family heirloom of nature vs. nurture,

a border between two bodies yearning to become one,

a home for your lover's smell,

a phantom pain of memory & loss,

a holding together of a beginning & an end,

a keeping you out of where you don't belong,

the organ of the body allowed to take up the most space.

HEALTH

I

IN MY FAMILY, the sick and the susceptible have never been allowed near the dying, because they—the women in particular—believe that somehow death is contagious. My first reason for this belief is due to the fact that as a child I was not able to attend my baby cousin's funeral. He was stillborn, and perhaps there was some superstition that if healthy breathing children attended another child's funeral, they would "catch death" and perish as well.

The second bit of evidence that lead me to this conclusion stemmed from the fact that in a Dominican family, it was customary to bring EVERYONE to almost EVERYTHING, including but not limited to birthday parties, anniversaries, sports games, performances, holiday celebrations, hospitalizations, weddings, funerals and, yes, even last moments. We were the type of people to do everything en familia. Unless, however, as was the case with me, you were either excused from or not "allowed" to attend certain family engagements because you were "la enferma."

The sick one in the family was allowed certain passes, like not being required to wash dishes in someone else's house after a dinner party or carry in heavy grocery bags. The sick one, who because she may end up on her own deathbed at any given moment, was also denied certain privileges, like sunbathing and too much wine or visiting a dying family member. Which is what happened to me when my uncle Daniel was dying of liver failure and when my Tía Morena was dying from lupus complications and pulmonary hypertension.

❧ ❧ ❧

A TV buzzed with the sound of a Mexican telenovela. A microwave beeped and a coffee machine gurgled with day-old coffee. Mami and I stood in an embrace. Mami wiped her eyes as if the tears that fell were a pesky fruit fly or a fallen eyelash.

"No es bueno para ti que lo veas así," she mumbled while fiddling with her short black split ends and sucking her teeth, annoyed that she has to have these conversations with me time and time again. Since my diagnosis, Mami had become an expert on things that were "not good for me."

Sitting in the sun.

Eating tomato sauce.

The cold.

The heat.

Milk products.

Caffeine.

Running and Zumba.

Sleepless nights.

Anger.

Stress.

Sadness.

Dying people.

At first, I thought Mami was trying to help preserve our dying loved one's memory. I thought Mami didn't want the image of who they were to be degraded by who they had become. I thought Mami was embarrassed for them. But when everyone else, including small children, the elderly and even the random church friend whose name no one remembers was allowed in the room to see said dying loved one, I realized this rule applied only to me.

Heels clicked in the hallway outside the waiting room. Mami sniffled and a water cooler vibrated nearby. I let out an uneven sigh as my breath stopped and hiccupped, a side effect of the fluid in my lungs from a lupus flare-up. My ribs were sore and my lung capacity weak from all the crying the night before. My uncle, my mother's brother-in-law, was in his final days, and we were all grieving.

I stood in front of Mami, trying to get past her to see him, but she would not let me.

"¿Pero por qué no lo puedo ver? Why not? He's not contagious, is he?" I asked with emotional and physical exasperation.

"No. Pero tú sabes. It's not good for you. Que te estrese . . . stress no good for you." Mami was thinking that if I got too close to Death, then Death would come for me next.

But I was not on my deathbed. Not yet. I did not have machines breathing for me or pumping my heart. I didn't need Mami to "protect" me from Death. I was fuming.

"Mami, please! Por favor, stop. I know what's good for me and what's not. I want to see him."

The buzzing room filled with machines and strangers, and everyone my uncle had ever loved, fell silent.

❧ ❧ ❧

As an only child, Lupe was not used to the way my family handled sick loved ones. In his small family of three, they also did things en familia, but they did it small and without much fuss. Birthdays involved quiet dinners or a modest BBQ on a Sunday afternoon. No birthday song or candles, maybe a bouquet of flowers for his mom, but not much else. If you were hospitalized, well that was an even quieter and quicker affair.

The first time I had to stay overnight in the hospital was right after Lupe and I had returned from our honeymoon in Punta Cana. I had been struck by chronic, debilitating, "feels like a kick to the back of the head" migraine. I thought it was the heat or the greasy food I had eaten. But when we got back to the States, the pain persisted. I was miserable for almost twenty-four hours a day. My head pounded and throbbed. I was consumed by dizzy spells and nausea, overwhelmed by hot flashes and cold sweats. It took one long, agonizing month of piercing and debilitating pain in my skull for my doctors to finally decide it was serious enough to run some tests and figure out what was going on. I was supposed to go in for an outpatient cerebral angiogram, in which they pumped iodine into my brain to "get a better view." What resulted was a three-night stay in the hospital because my blood pressure had spiked while in the recovery room, and I could have had a stroke.

After the ache in my cranium subsided and my team of doctors (a rheumatologist, a cardiologist and a neurologist) argued over what was wrong with me, they came to the conclusion that I was suffering from reversible cerebral vasoconstriction, that is, high blood pressure in the brain that would eventually go away and be fixed. It was also known as "thunderclap headache." My friends and I laughed a great deal about that term.

Once I was put on the right meds to combat the pain and pressure, I was allowed to eat and receive visitors. My parents were already in town because they had agreed to help us remodel our home. While my father stayed at the house and ripped up tile from our bathroom floor, like he wished he could rip this disease out of me, my mother paced the waiting room, pulled at the ends of her hair and said a hundred prayers to saints and angels who failed to work miracles. My mom would've stayed at my side 24/7 had Lupe not sent her home to get some sleep. A few friends came, and all my tías stopped by from San Antonio, a three-hour drive from Houston, just to say hi and wish me well.

As was expected, their "brief" hello turned into a four-hour conversation and a two-night stay at our house. My aunts and uncles and cousins came and went from the house to the hospital. They helped my parents remodel our kitchen, cook meals, wash our laundry and stifle their fear and sorrow with laughter, beer and loud merengues on the stereo. All that commotion and energy made Lupe anxious, since he wasn't used to such a hands-on approach to family love and concern. His family believed that the best you could do for someone who was ill was to just leave them alone.

While in the hospital, my in-laws stopped by my room for a grand total of forty-five minutes, and only because Lupe's mother helped me sponge bath. Yes, my mother-in-law, a woman whom I had only known by that title for two months, gave me a sponge bath. She was a retired nurse and loved me unconditionally. Lupe and I had dated for three years and been engaged for one before getting married, so she wasn't a stranger to me. I trusted her. She knew what to do.

While I felt even more comfortable with my in-laws by my side than I did with my aunts and cousins, Lupe's modest and humble parents did not want to impose on my recovery and refused to stay too long. I don't even remember his dad being there, because I was asleep when they first arrived, and by the time I woke up, he'd already left the room and was waiting outside in the car. They only came to ensure that I was still alive and on the way to health and healing.

During that first hospital stay, Lupe found it very frustrating and stressful to have all of my family around at the house and at the hospital. He wanted to be a good host to them and make them comfortable, but he was also trying to do his husbandly duties and take care of me. I didn't realize all this until after the fact, because I was in too much pain or so heavily medicated that I didn't know which way was up or down, much less what everyone else was feeling or doing. Since then, I've been hospitalized several times, and we have discussed whom, how and when family and friends are allowed to see me. Not so much because I care, but because Lupe needs his rest and his sanity when trying to manage my healthcare, when it's difficult for me to do it myself.

❧ ❧ ❧

So here I was, being one of those family members, who wants to see the patient, even if it's not in the best interest of the patient. Truthfully, although I knew everyone wanted to say their goodbyes, the last thing he needed was copious amounts of people entering and exiting his room. All that the dying want to do is to die. I knew this because as a sick person, all the sick want to do is be sick peacefully so they can get better quickly. Hard to do between the doctors and nurses checking in on you every thirty minutes so you can't even sleep. Even more impossible when your room is full of well-intentioned family members who shout when they speak and laugh robustly, despite hospital signs that request quiet rooms and silent hallways.

Nonetheless, I wanted my time to say hello and goodbye. Even if I knew he couldn't hear me because his heartbeat was governed by machines and his lungs inflated and deflated to the rhythm of a battery-controlled ventilator. I wanted to see him, even if I never really knew him growing up. I wanted to talk to him, even though I could count on one hand the number of conversations we had had. I wanted to be allowed into the room, if for no other reason than to be treated like everyone else and not like la enferma. After all, death wasn't contagious.

I tried to calm down and convince Mami with tenderness rather than anger. "Mami, you have to let me see him one last time. I won't stay in there long, I promise. Lupe can go with me, and if he thinks I need to leave, we'll leave. Okay?"

"Okay," she finally acquiesced.

I wiped her face clean of tears and grief and told her to sit down. I brought her some lukewarm water in a Styrofoam cup. She set the cup down without drinking from it, dug in her purse for her blue quartz-stone Rosary, closed her eyes, caught her breath and began to pray.

Lupe and I left the waiting room and found my four-and-a-half-foot aunt standing in the hallway outside my uncle's room. She was dressed in jeans and a navy T-shirt, her dark brown hair was pulled back in a curly ponytail and she had dark circles under her eyes. I could tell she hadn't slept for days.

"Hola, Tía," I said.

"Hi, Yamina. ¿Cómo estas?"

"I'm fine. How are you?"

"Bueno, ya sabes, más o menos."

"Can we go in and see him for a moment?"

"Claro que sí, of course."

She pointed us to a box filled with blue surgical masks on the wall outside his room and asked us to put them on for our protection and his.

"Okay. Gracias, Tía."

Lupe and I both grabbed a mask and walked into the room.

We stood near the doorway. I stayed close to Lupe, holding his forearm and trying desperately not to cry. My uncle lay in the hospital bed, waiting for the "go ahead" from the next of kin to unplug the machines and let him rest in peace. Swish. Beep. Pump. Buzz. I stared at my uncle without really seeing him. A blur. Skin. Bones. Cartilage. Tubes. The smell of rubbing alcohol in the room overwhelmed me. Swish. Beep. Pump. Buzz.

"Hola, Tío. It's me Jasminne," I said, my voice cracking. I held Lupe's arm tighter.

Swish. Beep. Pump. Buzz.

"I just wanted to tell you that I love you, Tío." I burrowed my head into Lupe's shoulder.

Swish. Beep. Pump. Buzz.

"Let's go, honey. It's not good for you to get like this," he said.

I didn't fight him, because I knew he was right. We left the room. The door clicked behind us. Lupe held me close.

"I love you," he whispered.

I cried. He held me closer.

❧ ❧ ❧

A couple of days later, whatever I had eaten wasn't sitting well. But I needed to get out of my head for a while, so Lupe had suggested going to a bookstore. As we entered, I caught the aroma of fresh-brewed coffee mixed with the inside pages of a musty old library book. The air was delicious and it gave me a buzz. My eyes felt heavy and the aisles were a blur. I didn't, we didn't, need any more books. But it felt like I was feeding a much-needed addiction, and I felt safe there. I felt like everything just might be okay.

I walked to the children's section. I was drawn to all the color. It felt joyful there, and I hoped joy was contagious.

"Look at me," said Lupe, grabbing my wrists.

"What? What is it?"

His olive skin and deep brown eyes came into focus. It was the first thing I was able to see clearly that day.

"Your mom wanted me to let you know that they took your uncle off life support today." He squeezed my hands. They began to sweat and he waited for a sign of understanding in my face.

"Oh." I pulled my hands back, looked up at the fluorescent lights that blurred my vision again and I grabbed a stuffed Curious George doll from the shelf and held it close. It was plush, soft and warm, like I imagined the warmth of a newborn baby to be. The store was cold. My fingertips began to tingle and ache from the chill. Something was burning in the café, and the hint of smoke made my eyes water. Two children ran past us, and I shivered watching them skirt the bookshelves. I had to lean on Lupe to keep from losing my balance. My stomach grumbled, and I clutched my belly with my free hand.

"Are you okay?" He reached for my elbow to steady me and tried to find my eyes.

"Yeah."

I couldn't look at him. My eyes just would not focus. I heard talking and laughing and someone reading to themselves. I closed my eyes, willing the tears to come, wishing in vain for grief to manifest itself into something I could understand or explain so I could cry. I found it hard to breathe. I held Curious George close and I let Lupe hold me.

II

When my aunt, Tía Morena, was in her last days, things were much the same when it came to Mami's overprotective nature, but that encounter with death and dying was different for all of us. It was different for Mami because this was the sister she helped my grandmother birth when Mami was only eight years old. She saw Tía Morena's head when she crowned and helped the midwife wipe the blood off her matted hair. And now in the final hours, it was Mami who would hold Tía Morena's hand in the middle of the night as her lungs gave out and God took over.

It was different for me, because while my uncle and I shared an understanding of chronic pain and illness, my aunt and I shared a diagnosis. Tía Morena's official cause of death was "heart failure due to complications from lupus and pulmonary hypertension." As someone living with lupus, I wondered if our death certificates would be carbon copies of each other.

Tía Morena's last days were spent in my mother's guest bedroom surrounded by her daughters, my grandmother and all my other tías. Nurses came and went around the clock, helping her dress, helping her eat, pumping her full of morphine and making her "as comfortable as possible." And while Mami wanted me to be able to say goodbye, she didn't want me to stay long because she didn't think it was good for me.

When I arrived at Mami's house, there was a flurry of activity. My aunts were in the kitchen cooking, chopping and chatting away in hushed whispers and stolen glances. As Lupe and I entered, the tension was palpable. The AC klicked on and the oven timer beeped.

"Oh, you're here, Yamina. Qué bueno," Mami said as she stretched out her arms to hug Lupe and me. "Look, we have arroz con pollo, your favorite," she said walking over to the stove and lifting the lid off the pot of rice.

"We already ate. Thank you, Ma." I hugged her again from behind, smelling her hair and squeezing her tight. "Can I see her now?"

"She's sleeping right now and . . . " Mami looked away.

"It's okay. I just want to see her. I don't have to talk to her or anything."

It was déjà vu. Like closing night of a terrible play you've over-rehearsed and no one came to. These were my lines, and I had to keep saying them in order for the show to go on.

Mami pulled at the ends of her hair and chewed off a piece. "Lupe, ve con ella, go in with her."

My mother's worry filled the room and suffocated us all. No one inhaled. No one exhaled. We all knew that at any moment, with the wrong look, the wrong word, the wrong gesture, this woman who stood as strong and as ominous as a dormant volcano could and would eventually implode and explode all at once. This was something no one wanted to be responsible for, but none of the family knew what to do.

So, in his usual gregarious and appeasing manner, Lupe, who was not blood-related and didn't carry our family's baggage, recited his usual well-rehearsed lines: "Of course, claro que sí, Mom. I'll go in with her. Whatever you want."

Mami half smiled and pulled at her hair.

Lupe walked into the room first, holding my hand as I stared at the newly remodeled floor, an obscure shade of walnut laminate.

Beep. Swish. Thump. Pump. Buzz.

I looked up. Tía Morena lay as still as the laminate floor. Her dark resilient skin, like the steady ground beneath my feet, an obscure shade of walnut.

Beep. Swish. Thump. Pump. Buzz.

"Hola, Tía," I whispered as gently as I could.

Her eyes opened and she smirked at me.

Yeah, I thought, she's still in there. Even without her red lipstick on and an oxygen tube instead of a cigarette in her mouth, she was still in there. Still sexy. Still flirty and fun. Still alive.

"¿Cómo me veo?" she asked and reached for my hand, winking and smiling even brighter than before.

"You look great, Tía." I squeezed her palm and sat down.

Beep. Swish. Thump. Pump. Buzz.

She closed her eyes and drifted off again. I stared at her, believing I would see my own reflection, afraid I was looking into a mirror twenty or thirty years down the road. But as I inched closer, I only saw her. Her closed eyelids, her delicately parted hair, her pale lips and her walnut-colored skin. Soon, her laughter would no longer vibrate in her chest and beckon men to come to her side. Soon enough, her pain and her memories of that suffering would evaporate as quickly as the condensation did from the glass of whiskey she drank one week before she died. Soon, our saying, "Tía Morena is" would become "Tía Morena was."

Beep. Swish. Thump. Pump. Buzz.

I saw a wave of peace wash over her. It filled me with joy.

"Gracias, Tía." I thanked her.

She didn't know why. Or maybe she did. I'm not sure. But I thanked her for showing me how simple and graceful dying could be. I thanked her for being beautiful until the very end. I thanked her for all that she had shown me in the past and all the lessons I would continue to learn from remembering her. I thanked her because, when I failed to see myself in her reflection, it reminded me that whether my end would come like hers was irrelevant. Death was inevitable. What mattered most was the journey.

Beep. Swish. Thump. Pump. Buzz.

Tía Morena coughed. I held my breath, and the room began to spin.

Lupe squeezed my shoulder and told me we should leave. I didn't fight him because, again, I knew he was right. I got up from the chair, knowing there would be no more red lipstick on my cheeks from her, no more winks to make me smile, no more cooking lessons or motivational speeches about how life was wonderful and to be lived fully. This was the last time I would see her, and so she smiled at me. It was contagious. I smiled back.

My tía Morena died quietly three days later, in the middle of the night with only my mother at her side. Mami says that when it happened, a glass vase holding a burning white candle shattered on the dining room table.

"POP!" she said it went. "Así, no más. Just POP!"

And there was glass on the floor and wax dripping everywhere and machines buzzing and Mami crying and Tía Morena lying there, still.

In her stillness we found grace. And grace was that gentle feeling, that moment of reprieve, the quiet understanding within the self that whispered in the soul and said, "She did the best she could, she woke up every day, and she tried."

HOME

A<small>FTER THIRTY-TWO YEARS</small> in the United States dedicated to the American Dream, Mami and Papi decided to emigrate back to the DR. Papi spent twenty-two years in the Army followed by almost ten years as an educator and then administrator in American public schools, along with taking classes on everything from advanced chemistry to accounting and childhood development, and was now embarking on a third career and a third degree in medicine. At the age of 63, Papi, had decided to pursue med school—in Santo Domingo. He chose Santo Domingo because he knew that his barely average English skills and faulty reading comprehension wouldn't allow him to be accepted into, much less successfully complete, a medical degree program in the United States. He had decided, without really consulting Mami or the rest of us, that the best place to achieve his last big dream was in the country of his birth.

No one in the family doubted that Papi could get accepted into medical school, and we knew he was smart enough to do so, but every time he brought it up, we rolled our eyes. We figured it was a pipe dream, a far-fetched fantastical idea, like the time he and Mami bought a time-share. We were sure this would not come to fruition and, even if he did actually attend, we knew it wouldn't be long before his brain gave out and he realized he wouldn't be able to keep up with the coursework.

I believed Papi didn't quite understand how med school worked. I tried to explain it to him based on my obsession with shows like *House*, *Grey's Anatomy* and *ER* and my many interactions with doctors and residents I'd had over the past few years

"Papi, med school isn't just four years of school, and then boom you're a doctor. You're going to have to get a residency somewhere, and that's like another two years. And then if you want to specialize in something like neurology or rheumatology, that's another four years on top of that. And then, because of your age, you're going to have a hard time finding a job."

He laughed at me and patted me on the back when I told him this. "Yamina, yo no me voy a sentar todavía. Mi mente está sana y lo voy a lograr." He told me he was not ready to spend the rest of his life sitting around on a beach or a golf course waiting on his retirement check to come in every month. He told me he knew it wouldn't be an easy journey, but he was excited and prepared for it, and that he didn't even want to practice medicine but that he still had a sound mind and he intended to use it.

No one actually believed he would apply to med school, get in and then leave his home, his kids and his life in the United States. We tried to convince him that the sacrifice was too much. We explained that at his and Mami's age, it was too much change and it would cost too much money to ship a car, buy new furniture, rent an apartment on the island, continue paying the mortgage on the house in San Antonio and cover all the bills and travel expenses. Papi wouldn't budge. When his acceptance letter came in, he renewed his Dominican and American passports, sold Mami's car and bought two one-way plane tickets to the island. Suddenly, it was no longer a joke, a pipe dream or a good laugh around the dinner table.

"What are you going to do with the house? You still have to pay the mortgage," my sister asked him one morning during a family breakfast after the Christmas holidays.

I had come in to San Antonio from Houston with Lupe. Jenny, twelve weeks pregnant with her first child, almost broke down into tears when she asked Papi about the house. She had recently revealed the news that she was pregnant and told Papi she couldn't fathom Mami not being by her side. Johnny, my sister's husband, stroked her arm and sighed. He too wanted my parents to stay in town because he enjoyed our family dinners and the generosity my parents had always shown him and his two sons from a previous relationship.

Papi was not as compassionate towards Jenny's emotional pleas. He giggled at her, put his fork down and very sincerely asked, "Well, do *you* want to live in it? Your mom and I don't want to leave it empty, and you have a big growing family. It's plenty of space for you, and I'd charge you less than what you're paying in rent right now."

Everyone at the table fell silent. My sister looked at her husband as if asking for help. He shrugged, indicating that the decision would be hers to make and kept eating his pancakes. Mami looked eagerly at Jenny, hoping and pleading with her gaze that she would say yes. I wanted to interject, but decided to stay out of it this time, so when everything hit the fan and my parents came back after a few failed months in the DR and my sister and her family had nowhere to live, no one could blame me and say it was all my terrible idea.

Jenny, realizing she would have to make this decision on her own cleared her throat and said, "No. No, Papi, I don't want to live there. The house is too big, it's too much for me to clean. I don't want to be responsible for it. Besides, that's not the point!"

She began to cry, which made us all uncomfortable. It was unlike Jenny to show so much emotion or to cry in public. I knew it was more than the hormones. No one wanted my parents to leave, even if they did annoy us sometimes.

"What is the point?" Papi asked without raising his voice or showing any indication that he'd been emotionally jarred by Jenny's sudden display of grief.

"Nothing, nothing. Never mind. Just do what you want. Haz lo que te dé la gana. I don't care anymore." She shook her head, pushed her plate away and took a sip of water.

I always hated seeing my little sister cry, because I knew if she did cry in front of anyone, she was hurting. I didn't want her to hurt, so I finally put in my two cents.

"Papi, Jenny is pregnant and she doesn't want to be alone. She wants Mami to be here with her along the way. It's a special time and it's not fair that all of a sudden you want to just pack up and leave."

"Your mother knows she can come back any time she wants and stay for as long as she wants. We've talked about it, and she'll be here for the baby shower and the delivery."

That's when Mami began to cry. Which broke me even further, and I had to swallow hard to keep my own tears from falling. The last few months of pleading and arguing and bargaining with Papi had been futile. He was set in his ways and had decided to do this with or without Mami. It was the first time in my life I had heard Mami speak of divorce. She had told us all, time after time, that she didn't want to leave her home, her kids, her grandkids, her friends and her sisters. She said she had planted roots in this country and everything and everyone she knew was in Texas. She had said over and over again, "Yo no tengo nada que buscar en Santo Domingo."

My heart ached for her. I wanted to fight to keep her in the home and life she had built. But Papi was a stubborn man, and now Mami, because she was his wife and she knew that her children were creating their own, had decided that despite the sorrow it caused her, she would go with him. Wiping the tears away, she came to his defense.

"Miren, yo sé que esto no es fácil para nadie pero . . . " She went on for about ten minutes telling us that Papi had spent the last thirty years of his life working with his hands and his heart to help *us* achieve our dreams. She said, he had put his life on hold to raise his kids and provide for our family. She said it was his turn now to achieve his dreams. I almost interrupted her when she said this because I thought he had come to the United States to pursue his dreams, not put them on hold. But before I could say anything, Mami continued with her defense.

"Al final del día, ya ustedes están grandes. Yo y tu papá solamente nos tenemos uno al otro."

Her voice cracked again, and I placed my hand on her back. She had finally voiced her truth. She was right, I thought: All they would have as they got older and all they had on a day-to-day basis was each other. My siblings and I had started our own lives and our own families. We still needed them, of course, but not like we used to. It was time for all of us to let go. But, we all know the real reason he had decided to pursue medicine, and because the guilt of my chronic illness has always kept me up at night, I tried one final approach to convince him to stay.

"Papi, please don't go to the D.R. Please don't leave us. We all need you both here. I know you want to help me. I know you want to learn as much as you can about my diseases. I know you want to try and find a cure. I know you are doing this for me. But, Papi," a high-pitched note escaped from the back of my throat and I almost didn't want to continue but knew I needed to say this now or I never would, "Papi, I don't need you to be my doctor. I need you to be my father."

Papi's face became stern and he broke into a half smile, his way of stifling grief and deflecting.

"Gracias," he said to all of us. "Pero ya tomamos la decisión. I'm going to medical school in Santo Domingo, and your mom and I are leaving." He looked away to indicate the topic was closed to debate.

A collective sigh of resignation engulfed us all. Silverware clinked against his glass plate, syrup stuck to his fingers, he took a swig of his orange juice. I had lost my appetite. I watched him eat and knew there was nothing more to say. In that moment, I accepted what we both knew to be true, that this grand gesture of returning home to find a cure, was the only way he knew how to be my father.

HAIMA

"WHAT FORM OF BIRTH CONTROL are you using?" Dr. Hassan asked, peering at me from above his glasses, his salt and peppered hair catching the light. He looked very handsome today, and his seemingly innocent, yet very loaded question made me smile.

"I'm not," I told him honestly.

He furrowed his brow and tapped his pen on the clipboard. "Why not?" He had told me for years to be on birth control, because the medications I was taking and my "very serious conditions could cause complications."

But having a child was what I dreamed about. I didn't want to resign myself to a life of childlessness. But I didn't tell him this. "Dr. Hassan, I don't want those hormones in my body. I don't even think I could get pregnant if we tried. I'm already taking too many pills. And honestly, I just don't feel like it."

All of this was true. Lupe and I had been trying to get pregnant for almost four years off and on, whenever my health seemed good enough. But it hadn't happened yet.

"You should not be getting pregnant," he said, fixing his white lab coat with authority.

I already knew this. I was aware of the risks. I could suffer from hypertension, preeclampsia, preterm labor, heart failure, kidney failure, blood clots, miscarriage and death. The medications I was on could cause birth defects or low birth weight. But even that wasn't enough to make me take the pill. I knew children with birth defects were hard to care for, but somewhere deep inside me, I believed God would know I had already been through enough, and if he allowed me to get pregnant, he would send us the child that was right for us.

I knew it was selfish of me to not be on birth control. I knew one of the reasons I even wanted to get pregnant was to prove that my body was capable of doing something right. But I also wanted to create a human being that would be part of me, part of Lupe, part of everything in between. I thought there was nothing more beautiful and honest than holding the hand of a living being who was created out of love. And even though I knew and understood the brokenness and toxicity of my body, I still had hope for it.

"Dr. Hassan, we've been trying for four years and we haven't gotten pregnant yet. Clearly, something is wrong. I'm not worried about getting pregnant." I was however, worried about why I couldn't get pregnant.

The "why couldn't I get pregnant" was the one thing my blood had not been able to reveal. My fertility bloodwork was always normal and high of the good stuff. My FSH was high, which meant I was fertile and there were no clear deficits in my egg count or quality. My blood was not clotting and had the right number of red and white blood cells. My blood could tell doctors when I had infections or inflammation, active disease or remission. But my blood could not tell me the only thing I wanted to know.

During the last few months thanks to the new treatment plan, all of my labs and tests were already showing improvement. My blood pressure was under control, the protein in my urine was lower and my bloodwork showed that the inflammation all over my body was lessening. I was also feeling better than I had in almost eight years. My joints didn't ache or swell. My shortness of breath and pleurisy had disappeared. I slept six to eight hours a night pain free, and I could do daily household chores as laundry, dishes and dinner all in one day rather than needing to pace myself throughout the week. I actually felt like I was living and not just surviving. I believed, for the first time ever, that remission was possible and that maybe in remission, my body would be strong enough and healthy enough to conceive and carry a child.

"Dr. Hassan, if I get pregnant, then I just get pregnant. We will cross that bridge when we get there. I know you can handle it. Besides, like I said, it hasn't happened after all these years, so I don't think we have anything to worry about."

His eyes widened behind his black-rimmed Versace glasses. "Don't you think that other seemingly infertile women have gotten pregnant 'by accident' after years of trying?" He raised his fingers in air quotes, and I knew he was scolding me again.

"I'm sure they have." The starchy paper on the clinic bed beneath me rustled. "But I'm leaving it up to God. If it happens, it happens, and we'll deal with it then." I smiled.

He laughed bewildered. "That's the worse use of God I've ever heard," he said. "God helps those who help themselves." He looked at me intently, like Papi used to when he was trying to make a point or give me advice he thought I shouldn't refuse.

"I'm sure you think so, and I know the risks, but I'm still not getting on birth control."

Over the years, Dr. Hassan and I had come to understand and respect each other. Our doctor-patient relationship consisted of him telling me what I should do and me deciding and taking the advice that suited me best.

I adjusted my clothing, hopped off the bed and grabbed my purse. "Thanks Dr. Hassan See you in three months."

He handed me the paperwork to get my labs done. We shook hands, and I left his office.

Downstairs at the phlebotomist's, I waited for my name to be called. I sat on a vinyl green chair, extended my right arm, let the phlebotomist search me for a reliable vein, pumped my fist several times, took a deep breath in when the needle punctured my flesh, and as I watched it flow into six different vials I would never see again, I knew that whatever story my blood told this time, it still wouldn't be the one I was longing to hear.

HOSTILITY

AFTER TRYING FOR FIVE YEARS to get pregnant with no success, Lupe and I decided to venture out to a fertility clinic to seriously consider our options. I was nearing thirty-two and I knew all the clocks were ticking. My fertility doctor, a handsome *Grey's Anatomy*-type man with thick blond hair and deep blue eyes, told me my infertility had to be treated aggressively.

After reviewing our records and lab results, Dr. Stuart told us, "It won't be easy for you to conceive. I recommend in-vitro fertilization. You could try other less invasive options, but there's less guarantee of success. IVF is the most aggressive treatment, but it gives you the best chances."

I sank into my seat and held back tears. This was not the first time I had needed aggressive treatment for a disease. Most of my scleroderma and lupus treatments were considered aggressive, but the ease with which he said the word—aggressive—as if he were giving me directions to the nearest gas station or ordering his daily cup of coffee, unnerved me and fluttered around in my brain.

We thanked Dr. Stuart and told him we had to consider all our options and would let him know what we decided in a few days.

"I don't know if I want to do this," I said to Lupe in tears on the way home.

"So we don't do it. It's fine. We don't have to do anything you don't want to. You're the one that will have to undergo the worst part of it, so I don't want you to do anything you're not comfortable with." He placed his hand on my shoulder. I rested my cheek on the warmth of his hand.

"But I want to give you a baby. I want us to have a family."

"We are a family. I have you and the dogs, and that's enough for me."

"But I don't want you to wake up five or ten years from now and resent me if I choose not to do this."

"I will never resent you. I love you. And we don't have to decide anything right now. Let's take a few days and see how we feel."

His words eased my fears but also made me feel more confused. If he had said he wanted a child more than anything, I would've signed up for IVF at that very moment. But he had left the decision up to me, and I knew my body had already been through enough.

That night, I lay in bed and wondered whose interests Dr. Stuart was pursuing, his or mine? Was he really trying to help me achieve my dream of becoming a mother? Or did he just want to assert his expertise on my body in order to increase and maintain his fertility success rates? I wondered if the answer even mattered. In the end, if I did conceive and give birth to a child, it would be a success for both of us. Right? Lupe and I were eager to start a family and carry on our legacy. But as an interracial couple we had fears about what our brown/black child might face growing up.

Police in America were more aggressive overall with African Americans and Latinos. Racism and violence against people of color had always been a reality for us, and I wondered if bringing a child into the world to be hated and feared was even worth it. We knew our future child, male or female, would face daily aggressions and aggressors. It was even possible that he/she would leave the world aggressively, and if it took aggressive treatment to give them life, what were their chances of survival outside the womb?

Before we received any "aggressive treatment" we had to find out what was causing our infertility. While the statistics stated that it was usually a combination of both male and female factors that led to infertility, I was sure, that given my medical history, I was the only one with the problem. I was also not optimistic that they would actually find anything wrong, since most of what was already wrong with me had no known cause or cure. But the tests were required, and I was willing to undergo all the testing needed if there was any chance we could find an answer that would lead to less aggressive treatment.

They began with bloodwork. The morning of the blood draw, I sat in the patient's chair, tilted my elbow in and clenched and released my fist, clenched and released. The needle pricked my median nerve #12 and I trembled.

"Relax" said the nurse in pink and purple scrubs, patting my arm with her blue-gloved hand. I did relax, because she was not aggressive.

After the blood draw, I was taken into a small exam room for a transvaginal ultrasound. I lied back on the table, covered my legs with a pink paper sheet, and placed my feet in the stirrups.

"You're going to feel some pressure," said the nurse as she inserted a large lubricated wand inside me. It was uncomfortable and cold, but the nurse was quick and gentle. She rolled the wand around from left to right to look at both of my ovaries.

"There are no immediate signs of aggressive cysts or fibroids, but I'll need to send these images to the doctor. He'll take a look at them and we'll call you in the next day or two with the results."

I sighed, closed my legs and sat up. "Thank you."

"From what I can tell, your ovaries look good. Relax. We'll see you soon."

A couple of days later, I had to go in for a hysteroscopy. This was the second most invasive "test." They put me to sleep and inserted a camera with a light inside my uterus in order to "look around." The procedure itself took less than half an hour.

While I was in the recovery room, Dr. Stuart came in to discuss what he had found. "Everything looks good. Your fallopian tubes are clear, and there are no signs of scarring. Everything looks healthy." He paused for a moment. "However, I did find some 'angry' tissue in your uterine lining. I've taken a biopsy of it to test for inflammation."

Of course my uterus was "angry," I thought to myself. It was being attacked. It was reddened and inflamed because it wanted to be left alone. It did not want to bring a child into this world under these aggressive conditions. It did not want to be prodded, penetrated, poked and studied under a microscope. It did not want to be questioned or threatened or subdued. All these years of trying and failing and testing had pissed my uterus off.

When the blood results, images and tests came back, everything checked out fine. I was slightly anemic, but that was expected, given my lupus nephritis. And while genetic testing showed that I carried the sickle-cell trait, Lupe wasn't a carrier, so that was not going to prevent us from trying. Otherwise, my egg count and quality was normal for my age, there were no cysts, fibroids nor abnormalities in my uterus, fallopian tubes or ovaries. And all of Lupe's tests came back normal too. So what was causing the problem?

At our follow-up visit to discuss the results, Dr. Stuart explained that we had unexplained secondary infertility, which was his way of saying what I already knew: I got pregnant once and never did again, and no one knew why. He said they would probably never know why because whatever was wrong, could not be diagnosed with the tests that currently existed. He insisted that our best chance at conception was IVF. It was not what either of us wanted to hear, but it was a reality we needed to accept.

A few weeks later, I sat at my best friend Camryn's house having a glass of wine in the middle of the afternoon. She was still on maternity leave and had invited me over after I told her the news about IVF. I was just now past the point of tears, and the wine was warming me up inside. She was always my biggest cheerleader in life, next to Mami, and she had been with me through everything during the last ten years. Ever the hopeful one, she asked, "So when you do get pregnant, what do you want? Boy or girl?"

"I used to say I wanted a boy because boys always love their moms best. But after Trayvon Martin, I started saying I wanted a girl. And then Sandra Bland happened, and I was even more confused. I wasn't so sure I wanted to have kids at all. But I've never stopped wanting to be a mom, no matter how hard I tried to make it go away."

I was almost in tears again, but I swallowed them down with another sip of wine. "I guess after all these years of trying, I just want the baby to be healthy and strong, no matter what it is. A baby is a baby. Whether it's a boy or a girl, it's still a lot of work."

"Cheers to that," she said and raised her glass. "Here, hold him," she said handing me her son to me after our toast. "You're going to need the practice."

I reached out and took him in my arms. I cradled him close to my breast and looked at his brown skin and brown eyes. His curly black hair rested on my elbow, and his face squished against my arm. I leaned in to kiss his soft fat cheek. My heart started to beat a little faster. I didn't want to want this, because the journey towards it had already been a long one. I didn't know how much strength I had left. But I also knew I couldn't just wish my dreams of motherhood away.

"So, what are you going to do?"

I held her son and watched his eyes discover my face, my hands and my smile. He hiccupped and smiled too. Suddenly, I knew I couldn't let my fears, or the world's hate win. I wanted to bring a child into this world as beautiful and as brave as him, as an act of resistance. And I knew that if my resistance was to be successful, it would have to be aggressive.

HERIDAS

I STARED AT THE SIX small scars on the outer part of my upper left arm and was reminded of the three skin biopsies my rheumatologist, Dr. Hassan, had performed on me as part of a medical research study. During my very first visit at his office, he asked me to participate in a study that he and his colleagues had embarked on to determine the cause and eventually a cure for scleroderma. I gave consent for my body to be an object of study because I wanted my illness to be of use to someone, even if that someone wasn't me.

❧ ❧ ❧

The skin of every piece of fruit is different. You can see where it's been bruised, beaten or punctured. If you squeeze the outer flesh, you can begin to understand the meaning of time. Too soon. Almost ready. Now. Too late.

A tip for picking mangos: A mango ripe for the picking will snap easily from its stem; if you have to pull too hard then it's not ready.

I jabbed my thumbnail into the side of a mango to diagnose its ripeness. I pinched out a small sample and confirmed that it was almost ready to eat. One more day and it would be ripe and sweet. But by then, my desire for the fruit would have subsided. My eagerness to indulge in a small taste of my childhood would be overshadowed by my to-do lists and responsibilities. If I didn't indulge in this delicacy right then and there, the mango would sit in a bowl on the counter for three more days, rotting and marking the passage of time until my fleeting appetite came back. By then, it would be too late, and I would be forced to throw both my desire and the mango out.

For years, I have allowed doctors and nurses to open my skin, take a piece and indulge in me until they were satisfied. My skin has been pierced by words, by needles, scalpels and syringes, by hot objects and cold hands. Some have left scars while others have been disappeared. All have been at my expense.

I peeled back the thin layer of the mango's dermis, and its secretions dribbled down my hands. I licked each fingertip, savoring the sticky sweet juice. Bright orange and yellow tender meat glistened and felt moist to my fingertips. I admired it for just one moment before taking a bite. More juice trickled down my chin. I slurped and inhaled with delight. My hands and wrists dripped with nectar. This moment was holy. The mango was a prayer in my mouth.

Mangos were first cultivated and grown in Southeast Asia over 4,000 years ago. They're shipped all over the world to countries where it's too cold for them to grow. They were first introduced in the Dominican Republic in the 1700s. Today, there are more than 130 mango varieties on the island.

Like the mango, there were pieces of me scattered all across Houston's medical center. Skin and kidney biopsies that could tell a stranger more about my body than I would ever understand about myself.

❧ ❧ ❧

On one of my visits back to the Dominican Republic as an adult, Mami and Papi took me to el campo. We drove on dirt roads, through hill country and along swamplands to visit the school they named after my grandfather, Angel de Jesús Durán, a man whose skin color I had inherited but never got the chance to touch. When he was alive, my grandfather was called "El Profesor" by the people of this small town. He was a respected teacher and community advocate and he loved his work. He used to bring the school kids breakfast and chocolate milk so they wouldn't go hungry during the day. He helped buy them shoes so they would be allowed in the classroom. When the townspeople decided to rebuild the local school, they remembered everything my grandfather had done for the village and decided to honor him for it. This school was his legacy and the only piece of him that remained.

Along the way, we stopped to buy mangoes from a street vendor. He handed me one that was ripe and sweet. I bit into it ferociously. I swooned. I slurped. Within seconds, my mouth erupted into tiny sores. My tongue itched, my throat swelled, I started hacking. Papi and the street vendor laughed while Mami stroked my back and handed me a bottle of water. I couldn't drink fast enough. I thought my lips and tongue would burst at the seams. I thought for sure this was how I would die. Death by mango. Once they pried the mango from my swollen hands and I was able to wipe my face and mouth clean of all the poisonous juices and mango remnants, the street vendor apologized. He said that the problem with picking mangoes right off the tree was that the skin carries an acid on them which, if not washed thoroughly enough, can burn.

✄ ✄ ✄

I have always wondered if the manifestation of scleroderma was my body's way of trying to protect me from the poisons of the outside world. When I asked Dr. Hassan to explain the results of my skin biopsies, the only thing I understood was that my body, my skin, was producing some kind of protein or substance it wasn't supposed to. He mentioned something about fibroblasts and keratin. He said that seven of the patients in the study, including me—regardless of age, sex or race—consistently had this protein substance show up in our biopsy results. He said this was a meaningful discovery and he was very excited about it. He said the results would be published in a medical journal. I asked him to send me a copy of the article when it came out. He did. And even though it was written in English, I didn't understand a word.

Once, I researched the different types of mangoes one could find in the DR. Some of the varieties I learned about included:

Gutoabajo—"goodness underneath/below"

Mariposa—"butterfly"

Sin sacar—"without removing"

Crema de oro—"golden cream"

I rolled the words around on my tongue and imagined how each of these mangoes would taste. Their names watered my mouth and felt round and rich with flavor. Their names, unlike the names of my diseases and all my symptoms, were not made in a lab or a hospital. Their names grew from the earth and fell from trees.

The first time I remember eating a mango, I was ten years old on a subway train in Nuremburg, Germany. Papi had picked up a couple of mangoes at the street market downtown and stuffed his pockets with the succulent fruit. It was winter, but somehow mangoes had found their way to Nuremburg and were now in the hands of my ravenous father. We sat on a train, and he pulled the mangoes out of his pockets. He stretched his hand out for me to see the bright orange beauty that made him giddy like a kid at Christmas. He pulled his Swiss Army knife out and sliced two tender oval pieces for me and for himself. Detached from its natural habitat, it looked vulnerable.

The golden sun-kissed flesh that rested beneath the mangoes skin mesmerized me. I stared intently as its natural pulp glistened beneath the train's fluorescent lights. I thought this must be the way fruit bleeds. I went to take a bite, but Papi told me to wait and watch him first. He took one slow Holy Communion bite of the sweet flesh, and I watched as the juice slid down his chin and onto his hands. He sucked and smacked his fingers, his lips and his teeth. Every moment and every drop of the sticky sweet juice was savored and held in his mouth like a blessing. I took my first clumsy bite and felt the meat of the mango burst with the flavors of an island I had never been to, but I understood its history and what Papi meant when he said, "This, this tastes like home."

꿏   꿏   꿏

The skin   I was born   lives in   the stories
        la piel
biopsy   take   sin sacar   remove   impede

        my flow   every direction   Yo nací.
I was born   como crema de oro
        black   Latina
        thick-skinned   la piel   changed   was reborn
became   el gutoabajo   la mariposa
            the moment   the world
the breath   underneath.

HEROINE

IT WAS VALENTINE'S DAY. Día del amor, la amistad y el corazón. Lupe and I had nothing planned this year since it was also just a Tuesday. That morning, Lupe had left early for work, and I snuggled under the covers, listening to the rain fall outside my window. I had fallen back asleep after he kissed me on the cheek, and by the time I woke up, I had overslept.

Late for work, I scurried to get ready. I grabbed my bags and bolted out the door. When I got in my car and turned the key, the gas light came on. I didn't really have time to get gas but I knew I wouldn't make it all the way to work. I drove to the gas station across from the railroad tracks near my house.

As I pulled up to the pump, the once soothing rain had begun to thrash against everything in its way. I rushed out of my car and ducked my head under the pump's barely-there awning. As I was unscrewing the gas cap, a petite middle-aged Asian woman in pink scrubs approached me from the opposite side of the pump. I was annoyed with her even before she began to speak because I was running late and didn't have time for whatever it was she wanted.

She held her shoulder and was breathing heavily. She leaned in and said, "Excuse me."

I furrowed my brow and turned my head to the side and said, "Yes?"

Her voice shook like the train that passed behind us in the background. "Can you please call 911?"

I looked around in a panic, hoping not to see blood anywhere. I grabbed my phone on instinct, because I had been this woman before. Only a few months after my first near-stroke and pericardial effusion, I had found myself stuck on the side of the road with heart palpitations and shortness of breath. I knew what it was like to be stuck on the side of the road, afraid of a heart attack and in need of medical help.

I dialed 911 and it rang. I walked around to where her car was parked and saw her leaning against it trying to breathe.

"Can you tell me what's wrong? What are you feeling?" The phone continued to ring.

She clutched at her collar. "My heart is beating really fast. I feel dizzy. I can't breathe."

She stumbled a bit. With my free hand I helped her open her car door and told her to sit down. I stood beside her car door and waited underneath the awning of the gas pump, listening to the phone ring. Gusts of rain continued to pelt my face and arms.

When the 911 emergency dispatch finally answered, she asked me if I needed medical, fire or police. I asked for medical, and she put me on hold.

The woman in the car was shaking her head and rubbing her hands.

"No, no, no," she kept repeating.

My own breath became short.

"What's wrong?" I asked.

She reached for her face. "I think my face is going numb."

I steadied my own breath before speaking so as to try and keep her calm and focused. "Okay. Just breathe in and out slowly for me. That's it. Just nice and slow."

I breathed in and out with her for her benefit as much as my own.

Moments later, a new dispatch answered and asked me for a name, phone number and location. I pulled the phone away from my mouth for a moment.

"Ma'am, what's your name?"

"Sylvia," she said between an inhale and an exhale.

I told the dispatch her name and gave the address of the gas station off the freeway. They asked me what her symptoms were, and I told them. They instructed me to keep her awake and to not let her fall asleep. They told us to stay put, because the EMTs would be there soon. I got off the phone and asked her if I could sit in her passenger's seat, because I wanted to comfort her and I needed to get out of the rain. She said yes, and I got in her car.

By this point, I realized that I would not make it to work on time, if I would even make it at all. I was only assigned to teach for two hours this morning and was already fifteen minutes behind my normal schedule. I decided to send a quick email on my phone to let the school know that I was dealing with an emergency situation and I would not make it into work. I could feel my own anxiety bubbling beneath the surface. This moment was triggering memories of my own near heart failure. I anticipated that when this was all over, and the adrenaline had subsided, my body would collapse and I wouldn't be able to function, much less teach for the rest of the day.

I knew it was important to keep Sylvia awake. And I might have to answer questions about her if she was unable to do so when the EMT arrived. So I started to ask her questions.

"Do you take any medications? Or have any medical problems?"

Her throat tightened when she began to speak. "I have high blood pressure and anxiety. But I know what tachycardia from my anxiety feels like and this is different." Her eyes rolled into the back of her head. She swallowed hard and rubbed her hands together.

My concern for her intensified. I knew my own blood pressure was probably climbing. I breathed in and out with her and decided to tell her my story.

"I know how scary this can be. I live with lupus and have had heart problems in the past. I've had to call 911 from a gas station parking lot too. I thought I was having a heart attack." I stopped mid-sentence because I realized that I was probably making her feel worse. She didn't need to hear about my near-death experience in the middle of what might be hers.

"It's going to be okay. The EMT will be here soon. Just breathe nice and slow."

The rain continued to beat down on us. We breathed in and out. "I'm worried about my car," she said. "I don't want to leave it in the parking lot. I don't want it to get towed or broken into."

I empathized with her. Her concerns did not surprise me. When I had left my car at the gas station, after the ambulance had picked me up for tachycardia, shortness of breath and hypertension, all I could think about was my car. I had also hoped it wouldn't get towed or broken into. At the time, I wasn't focused on heart failure. I was worried about my damn car, just like Sylvia. It must've been a way to deflect from the severity of the experience at hand.

I wanted to put Sylvia's mind at ease. So I asked her if there was anyone I could call for her. If there was anyone that could come to be there with her or pick up her car.

"I live with my mom, but she is very old. I take care of her. My cousin is off work today and can come get the car."

"Great. What's the number?"

She gave it to me, and I dialed it. The other line rang and rang but no one answered

"No one is answering. I'll try again in a few minutes." I put the phone down. "Do you live far from here?"

"No. I was on my way to work and I started to feel bad, so I pulled over. I was feeling just fine this morning. I was fine. I was fine." She shook her head. "Although I haven't taken my blood pressure medicine the last few days. I just forget, you know?" She shook her head again as if disappointed in herself. "I should've brought it with me."

"Don't worry. This isn't your fault. Don't worry, the ambulance will be here soon. Just breathe."

I breathed with her. The rain became a thunderstorm.

Moments later we heard sirens approaching. The wind and the rain began to flood everything around us. Gusts of wind and rain swirled around the car. It felt like we were being stirred inside a cup of seltzer water. My head began to swim. Sylvia's tiny white Chevrolet rocked side to side. I watched an empty black trashcan tap dance and roll across the gas station parking lot. Thunder pounded in the sky as the ambulance pulled up next to Sylvia's car.

"I don't think I can walk," she told me, rubbing her left thigh. "I can hardly feel my legs. What do you think is going to happen to my car?" Her voice cracked.

If she started to cry, I knew I would too, so I interrupted her to save us from the watershed of tears we both had bubbling up.

"Leave your keys with me. I'll move your car to a parking spot."

"Okay." She handed me her keys as three male EMTs approached the car.

It was hard for them to get too close to her car because she had pulled up close to the gas pump. They knocked on the window and she lowered it. One of the men barraged her with a series of questions.

"Ma'am, can you get out of the car?" Sylvia shrugged. "Can you move?"

"Yes."

"Does your chest hurt?"

"Yes."

"Can you take a deep breath?"

She tried. "No."

"Can you smile?" Her smile was weak.

"Ma'am, look at me. I'm trying to see if you are suffering a stroke. Look at me, please, ma'am, and smile if you can." She lifted her head at him and smiled.

"Can you get out of the car on your own?"

"I don't know."

My own heart began to beat even faster. I remembered the fear I felt in my own body when the threat of having a stroke loomed over me. I remembered these questions and their implications on the rest of my life. I wanted Sylvia to be fine and I didn't know how to help her.

The EMT cocked his head, narrowed his eyes as if he were searching her body for clues, and asked her accusingly, "Do you suffer from anxiety?"

Something inside me snapped. Even if Sylvia wasn't having an anxiety attack, I sure as hell was. Why didn't he believe what she was saying? And if it was an anxiety attack, how did that make her symptoms any less serious? What was the purpose of that question? Would he have asked a man that question? This EMT was wasting valuable time, and I wanted to come to her defense, but I didn't know what to say. I darted my eyes in his direction, hoping he could feel my fury. Hoping the wind and the rain would beat down on his smug face the way I wished I could. Before I could speak, Sylvia answered his question.

"Yes, I have anxiety, but this is not an anxiety attack. This feels different. I know what an anxiety attack feels like. This is not that." She stared straight ahead and clutched the neckline of her pink scrubs. She blinked hard and tried to catch her breath.

The EMT finally decided to open the car door and helped her into the ambulance. The ambulance door closed behind them. Another EMT tech came to the car and asked me for her purse. I handed it to him and got out of her car. What would happen to her car, I thought? I had left her keys in her purse. I couldn't park it, as I had told her I would. I felt bad that I had broken my promise.

When I got to my car I was soaked. My jeans were heavy from the rain, my socks were cold and my glasses steamed. I didn't know what else to do. I stared at the EMT van, with its lights flashing and the door closed. I wondered what they were doing to Sylvia and if she'd be all right.

The pelting rain intensified. Stop signs began to dance, and streetlights swung back and forth. I jumped at a clap of thunder. I looked to my left and my right and saw cars coming and going. I couldn't move. I didn't know which way to go. My vision blurred and my chest tightened. I wanted to head back across the railroad tracks to my house and curl up under the covers. I wanted to forget this feeling, but I knew that wouldn't help anyone. I gripped the steering wheel. I was trying to decide what to do, where to go. I noticed my face was cold and wet. I didn't know if it was from the rain or my tears. I wiped my cheeks and placed my hands on my heart. I clutched the collar of my shirt and began to sob.

I wanted to do more for Sylvia and for myself, but I was help-less. I wanted to move her car but I didn't have the keys. I wanted to pick up her mom and cousin and take them to the hospital, but I didn't know where they lived, and calling them to ask made me feel uncomfortable. More than anything, I wanted to stand up for Sylvia (but probably more for myself) and knock the wind out of the EMT guy so he knew what this gasping for air felt like. I wanted to tell him that our symptoms were real, that we knew our bodies better than anyone else and that no one had the right to negate the reality of our pain.

Sylvia's life was out of my hands. I had done what I could to help her, and that had to be enough. I decided to focus on the flashing red lights of the EMT van and breathe slowly until the ambulance drove off and my anxiety settled. I had to believe she would survive, if only because I had.

Later that night, I got a phone call from her cousin, who found my number on the caller ID. Sylvia had asked her to call me.

"Thank you for helping Sylvia today. She wanted us to let you know that she is going to be fine. She just had a bit of high blood pressure, but she is already home and resting. Thank you again."

"No problem. I'm glad that she's feeling better."

"God bless you," she said and hung up the phone.

I started to cry. I thought about Valentine's Day, and heart failure, and love, and friendship. I thought about how my own heart had almost failed me before, but that it was that same heart that had saved someone today. Sylvia was a stranger, but I had treated her with love. That's all any of us could ask for.

I placed my palms over my heart and felt it beating. I was still alive. Sylvia was still alive too. I never meant to be anyone's hero. I never asked to be on this journey. But perhaps I had had to suffer in order to be the person who pulled up next to Sylvia, who knew what to do, what to ask and how to spot the symptoms in order to help save her. If that was true, then everything I had endured and survived had been worth it.

ACKNOWLEDGEMENTS

Special thanks to the following publications where some of these essays and poems first appeared in various forms:

"Loss" was published under the title "I Miss You" in the anthology *Impact: A Collection of Short Memoir*, Telling Our Stories Press, 2012.

"Not Yet" was published in in the anthology *Reverie: Ultra Short Memoir*, Telling Our Stories Press, 2013.

"Shades of Red" was published by DangerousWoman Project.org, The University of Edinburgh, April, 2016.

"Dar a Luz" was first published in *Gulf Coast: A Journal of Literature and Fine Arts,* Winter/Spring 2018.

"Hands: El Corte" was published under the title *El Corte/The Cutting* and selected as honorable mention for the Barry Lopez Creative Non-Fiction prize for *The Best of Cutthroat: A Journal of the Arts*, March 2016.

"Morir soñando" was published in *Label Me Latina/o Special Issue: Black and Latin@: Conceptualizing Afro-Latinidad in Afro-Latina/o Literature and Performance,* Summer, 2017 Volume VII.

"Gluttony" was published in *Rogue Agent Journal*, Issue 27, June 2017.

"Heart" was published in *Chiricú Journal: Latino/a Literatures, Arts & Cultures,* Fall 2017.

GRACIAS

FIRST AND FOREMOST I would like to thank my parents Benjamin and Sonia Rosario-Sosa who gave me life and have never left my side throughout this journey and for being my biggest fans. Mil gracias to my husband Lupe to whom this book is dedicated because without him I would never have survived these illnesses or finished the book. You pushed me even when I didn't want to be pushed and didn't think I had the strength to keep going. I am also forever indebted to my in-laws, Pedro and Eusebia Méndez, whose love and support the last twelve years has been unwavering. Thank you to my sister Jennifer, and my niece Brooklyn for encouraging me and for always bringing me joy.

This book and my journey towards wellness would not have been possible without the wonderful medical staff at UT Physicians, most especially Dr. Shervin Assassi for saving my life on more than one occasion and always treating me with kindness and respect. Thanks also to Dr. Donald Molony, Dr. Pushan Jani, Dr. Carlos Hamilton and nurse Terry. Special thanks to my cardiologist Dr. Nishakawa at Memorial Hermann for taking care of my heart and believing in alternative medicine. A great and heartfelt thanks to my hand doctor Dr. Korsandi for saving my fingers from further amputation. Thank you to my acupuncturists Chris Axelrad and Susan Underwood, for helping me when western medicine couldn't. And thank you to my yoga teacher Rhia Robinson for helping me understand that my body was still capable of greatness.

I wanted to send a special shout out to my writing familia at Canto Mundo, Macondo and the Afro-Latina Writer's Retreat for helping me believe in myself as a poet and a writer and creating a community I fit into and can count on. Huge thanks especially to my VONA family, Sevé Torres, Jani Rose, Paula Paz, Tyrek Green, Rashaad Thomas, Willie Perdomo, Arielle Diaz, Lis White, Carlos Andres Gomez, Yein Kim and Tatiana Figueroa for being the light at the end of a very dark tunnel and for reminding me why I need to keep writing. Thank you to all the writing mentors and friends that read some of these essays and poems and provided feedback including, Molly Spencer, Raina Leon, Elizabeth Acevedo, Rosebud Ben-Oni, Deborah D.E.E.P Mouton, Icess Fernandez, Gauadalís del Carmen, Alicia Anabel Santos, Marilou Razo, Leslie Contreras Schwartz, Yesenia Montilla, Trevor Boffone and Claire Massey. Thank you also to the editors and staff at Arte Público Press for believing in this book and helping me turn it into something special.

Special thanks also goes out to the folks at the Rainier Writer's Workshop where many of these essays finally found their way thanks to my incredible mentor Barrie Jean Borich who never let me forget that I didn't have to give up being a poet to write a memoir. And thank you also to Rick Barot for believing in my work and advocating for me when I couldn't find the words, and thank you to Lena Khalaf Tuffaha, Jeric Smith, John Abasi, Libby Hall, Rigoberto Gonzalez and Camille Dungy for pulling me out of the dark places and reminding me of my purpose and strength.

I am eternally grateful to the many friends and family that have supported my writing journey and have made their way to my hospital bedside at one time or another including: Jon and Emily Ufer, Marina Pakkath, Hana Boston, Saul and Viv Belza, Angie and Joe Garcia, Dan Garcia, Camryn and Adam Wells, Ivy and Georgette Greene, Sabina Delgado, Mirian Nuñez Florentino, Jennifer Sommers, Hannah Adair Bonner, Blanca Alanis, Abigail Suzahns, Ruby Rivera, Alicia Jones, Karima Wilson, mi abuelita Mama (QDEP), and mis tías Daveyba, Amaryllis, Maria and La Morena(QDEP).

Last but certainly not least, this book was written for all the scleroderma and lupus warriors out there that are surviving and thriving each and every day. The love and support and strength my chronic illness family has shown me over the last ten years is unparalleled and this book was written so that our stories could be heard. Finally,

I'd like to thank the Scleroderma Foundation Texas Bluebonnet Chapter and the Lupus Foundation Texas Gulf Coast chapter for providing me with the resources and support I needed to get through the most difficult times and make it to where I am today.